Los Angeles Public Branch
Social Science/Philosophy
& Religion Dept.
630 W. Fifth Street
Los Angeles, CA 90071

MAR 2 2 2007

W9-AUI-121

WITHDRAWN

WITHDRAWN

Open for Debate
Media Bias

L.A. PUBLIC LIBRARY - SOCIAL SCIENCE/PHIL/REL

Open for Debate

Media Bias

Tom Streissguth

301.55
S915-1

mc Marshall Cavendish
Benchmark
New York

APR 1 6 2007

Marshall Cavendish Benchmark
99 White Plains Road
Tarrytown, NY 10591-9001
www.marshallcavendish.us

Copyright © 2007 by Marshall Cavendish Corporation
All rights reserved. No part of this book may be reproduced or utilized in any form or by any
means electronic or mechanical including photocopying, recording, or by any information storage
and retrieval system, without permission from the copyright holders.

All Internet sites were available and accurate when sent to press.
Library of Congress Cataloging-in-Publication Data
Streissguth, Thomas, 1958-
Media bias / by Tom Streissguth.
p. cm. — (Open for debate)
Summary: "Discusses bias in the American media, including its historical development and the
effects of new technologies. Includes discussions of different types of bias, government regulations,
politics, and public relations, and how they shape the media"—Provided by publisher.
Includes bibliographical references and index.
ISBN-13: 978-0-7614-2296-9
ISBN-10: 0-7614-2296-X
1. Mass media—Social aspects—United States. 2. Mass media—Political aspects—
United States. 3. United States—Politics and government—Press coverage. 4. Mass media
and public opinion—United States. I. Title. II. Series.

HN90.M3S83 2006
302.230973—dc22
2005037560

Photo research by Linda Sykes Picture Research, Inc., Hilton Head, SC

Alamy: cover; georgewbush.com/ Reuters/Corbis: 6; The Granger Collection,
New York: 15, 18, 21; Richard Ellis/Corbis Sygma: 30; Reuters/Corbis: 38, 74, 85, 105;
Steve Marcus/Reuters/Corbis: 42; Bettmann/Corbis: 49; Lou Dematteis/Reuters/Corbis: 52;
Najiah Feanny/Corbis Saba: 61;Richard Ellis/Corbis Sygma: 62; Corbis Sygma: 66; Eliana Aponte/
Reuters/Corbis: 77; Arko Datta/Reuters/Corbis: 87; Ajmal Baheer/Reuters/Corbis: 88; Janes
Leynse/Corbis: 95; Vaughn Youtz/ZUMA/Corbis: 99.

Editorial Director: Michelle Bisson
Art Director: Anahid Hamparian
Series Designer: Sonia Chaghatzbanian

Printed in China
1 3 5 6 4 2

Contents

ADVERTISEMENTS ARE PRIME MEDIA MANIPULATION TOOLS DURING POLITICAL CAMPAIGNS. THIS AD FOR THE BUSH-CHENEY 2004 CAMPAIGN "HIJACKS" THE OLYMPICS BRAND, LEAVING OFF ITS FIVE OLYMPIC RINGS, BUT ADDING "120 DEMOCRACIES" AS AN ANNOUNCER TELLS VIEWERS THAT "AT THIS OLYMPICS THERE WILL BE TWO MORE FREE NATIONS," REFERRING TO THE U.S.-LED INVASIONS OF AFGHANISTAN AND IRAQ.

Introduction

News and entertainment media play a very important role in contemporary life. The leisure time of millions of people is devoted to paying attention to the media, in the form of broadcasting (television and radio), text (newspapers, magazines, and books), and the Internet. An army of technicians, managers, writers, editors, and broadcast personalities deliver this content to its consumers. Politicians and organizations make constant use of the media, carefully shaping the public perception of their ideas and products. An entire profession of public relations revolves around the skillful use of the media to sway public opinion and boost sales.

The money and power at stake in the media business are huge. Billions of dollars are spent on advertising in the media, and many billions more are spent by media companies to produce and deliver content to the consumer. Broadcast licenses issued by the federal government are coveted by private companies. Newspapers printed in the media capitals—Washington, D.C., New York, and Los Angeles— are distributed all over the country. The information media loom over modern society, and especially its political life, with a reach unmatched by any other institution.

By the same token, the media have the effect of making individuals feel small and insignificant. The power to broadcast and publicize events dwarfs any individual's efforts to make a difference in such a large and diverse society. Televisions are in every home, in public places, in stores, in restaurants, in automobiles, and on airplanes. The electronic and print media are intrusive and inescapable. As a result, those who watch and read often feel suspicious about the media's true intentions and motivations. The sensational nature of major media stories, and the pervasive presence of television, cause a strong reaction in people.

As a result, many people see bias and unfairness in the media. In the first years of the twenty-first century, the focus of the media-bias debate was on the U.S. occupation of Iraq. Conservatives point out the negative coverage of President George W. Bush and media stories about the war he initiated in March 2003. In their view, media war stories emphasize death and bloodshed, while playing down positive effects of the war, such as democratic votes for a new Iraqi president and constitution. Liberals generally opposed to Bush have an opposite reaction. They see the media glorifying the war with colorful maps, exciting video footage, and dramatic stories about heroes and rescues. They look in vain for stories that show the war's violence and futility, as well as the strong opposition to the occupation among everyday Iraqi citizens.

Accusations of bias are often a cover for someone's attempt to sway public opinion. By pointing out a slanted newspaper article or television report, a politician can show that his or her own side has been treated unfairly, and raise the public's sympathy for that point of view. Stories of media bias have become a staple of media content as each side carefully and thoroughly points out how its views get an unfair treatment, how corporations or the government are in control, how reporters are naturally inclined one way or the other, how laziness has allowed falsehood to get into print, or how televised images trivialize important events. On many networks and in printed sources, unfair bias is simply assumed and goes unchallenged. It is far easier to make accusations of bias than it is to prove them wrong, and far easier to spread a rumor of bias than to report carefully verified facts.

The emotional attachment people have to their political views makes a clear-eyed look at a given issue hard to achieve. By assuming bias on the part of the media, those without strong political views one way or the other become cynics, while the subject of bias reinforces the public's mistrust of large and powerful institutions. The effect is to confirm the natural suspicion that people have toward their leaders and government.

There is no solution to the problem of media bias. Nor are we likely to resolve the debate, one way or the other. As long as people hold opinions, those opinions will color the bent of articles in newspapers and reports on television. Media bias is a product of these opinions and, among consumers, a matter of perception—and individuals often disagree on their perceptions. Proof is another matter, and in the end impossible to achieve. The media have grown too large and varied to generalize about. The debate will go on, even as the Internet and other new technologies bring about an information transformation in the twenty-first century.

American Media: A Biased History

In September 1690, Boston became the first city in the North American colonies with a newspaper, *Publick Occurrences Both Forreign and Domestick*. This paper was edited by Benjamin Harris, a Londoner who had fled to the colonies after his accusations of Catholic plots against the English government landed him in jail. *Public Occurrences* was intended as a platform for Harris to air his strong prejudices against Catholics. But, to the powers that be, such a publication posed a threat to civic order. Immediately after *Publick Occurrences* appeared, the newspaper was banned by the governor. Only one edition ever appeared.

In 1704 the *Boston News-Letter* appeared, followed by the Boston *Gazette* in 1719 and the *New England Courant* in 1721 (edited by James Franklin, the older brother of Benjamin Franklin). Pamphlets and broadsides (one-page newspapers) also appeared, distributed freely or sold for a pittance. In colonial times, these were the most common means of expressing and debating political ideas. Every newspaper and publication had a political slant that was well-known to the reading public.

The reason for this bias was financial. There was little money in the colonies, or in the early United States, for printing. Neither advertising revenues nor money from subscriptions covered expenses. Newspapers depended on patronage from political parties to survive. Their articles were meant to show these patrons in the best possible light, and to make rivals look bad. "The results," comments author Darrell West, "were low subscription levels, lack of reader respect, and an eighteenth-century media with very limited independent power. Citizens read papers with which they already agreed or relied on more than one paper to obtain a balanced point of view."

Jefferson and Callendar

The British colonies rebelled in 1775 and won their independence after chasing the British army from North America. By the Constitution's First Amendment, freedom of speech and assembly were guaranteed. There would be no interference in free expression by the government. Citizens were given the right to gather in public places and express their views openly. Newspapers could print their opinion and express their bias, either in support of or in opposition to the government and political parties, without fear of government action against them.

The editors of the young republic were not afraid to show their partisan bias. They enthusiastically printed personal information, spread rumors and gossip, and speculated on the private lives of public figures. They also fomented scandal when they believed it would help their side. One of the most prominent victims of such a media scandal campaign was Thomas Jefferson.

As the third president and the author of the Declaration of Independence, Thomas Jefferson was widely revered as a founding father of the United States. But he was also widely reviled for his politics. The leader of the Democratic-Republican Party, Jefferson believed in democracy. He had no use for the Federalists, who favored a strong central government. He didn't care for city people or merchants. The yeoman farmer, the man who tilled the soil and supported his family from the land's natural bounty, was Jefferson's ideal man. He believed the states should be largely independent, write their own laws, protect their own borders, and act with only their own residents' best interest in mind.

Opponents saw Jefferson as a dangerous radical, a man set on breaking up the republic, attacking the wealthy, and fomenting political chaos. The presidential election of 1800 saw anti-Jefferson newspapers flinging every sort of accusation at their target, including allegations that he had sexual relations with his slaves.

The mudslinging was brought to a fever pitch by a publisher named James Callendar. Once a political ally, Jefferson had used Callendar to whip up scandals against the president's many rivals, including John Adams and Alexander Hamilton. But Callendar felt slighted when Jefferson did not offer him a good job in his new administration. He turned against his former patron with a vengeance. The campaign began with columns criticizing the president's policies, then went on to more personal attacks:

> **It is well known that a man whom it delighteth the people to honor, keeps and for many Years has kept, as his concubine, one of his slaves. Her name is SALLY. The name of her eldest son is Tom. By this wench**

> **Sally, our president has had several children. There is not an individual in the neighbourhood of Charlottesville who does not believe the story. . . . Mute! Mute! Mute! Yes very Mute! Will all those republican printers of biographical information be upon this point.**

Although the rumors may have been true, the Callendar campaign had little effect. Callendar drowned in a shallow stretch of the James River in 1803—the victim of an accident or, as some whispered, a murder. Jefferson was reelected by a wide margin as president in the next year.

The Penny Press

In these times, very few people read newspapers. Literate and educated people made up a small segment of the population. Reading was an occupation of the leisure class, and most families did not own books. Further, newspapers did not have strong influence over their political views or over government. People allied themselves with local politicians who addressed their immediate concerns. Party affiliation on the part of these politicians was an afterthought. Nor did elected officials pay much attention to the press. There were no publicists or agents working for politicians to give them a favorable slant in the press.

But newspapers began to multiply in the early nineteenth century. More people were reading newspapers as well as books and pamphlets. To support their operations, newspapers came to rely on regular subscribers, who received the newspaper through the mail or at their home. Literacy was increasing, lecture halls were filled, public debates between political candidates well attended. Writing in the 1830s, the French visitor Alexis de Tocqueville observed the importance of the press in America: "Its eyes are never shut, and it lays bare the secret shifts of politics, forcing public figures in turn to appear before the tribunal of opinion."

An important change came to the press with the appearance of the *New York Sun*, founded by Benjamin Day in 1833. The *Sun* and papers like it sold for a penny, making them affordable to a wider audience. The "penny press" shied away from political debate. Instead, these papers carried news of the day—the more sensational, the better. Reporters strived for hard-hitting, exciting stories—crimes of passion, lurid scandals, duels, and other affairs of honor. These melodramas echoed the plays that provided entertainment for the urban working class. Their basis in fact made them even more compelling to the average reader.

Media critic Neil Gabler, in *Life: The Movie: How Entertainment Conquered Reality*, comments that:

> **The single most important attraction of the penny press may have been the most obvious one—namely, that for a constituency being conditioned by trashy crime pamphlets, gory novels and overwrought melodramas, news was simply the most exciting, most entertaining content a paper could offer, especially when it was skewed, as it invariably was in the penny press, to the most sensational stories. In fact, one might even say that the masters of the penny press *invented* the concept of news because it was the best way to sell their papers in an entertainment environment.**

James Gordon Bennett founded the most successful penny newspaper, the *New York Herald*. In 1836, the *Herald*'s coverage of the murder of Helen Jewett, a twenty-three-year-old prostitute found axed to death in her bed, made the paper notorious. The newspaper carried lurid details of Jewett's troubled life and disturbing descriptions of the bloody murder scene. But the treatment of the story by the *Herald* caused a reaction from critics decrying its vulgar sensationalism. Civic leaders, politicians, and guardians of public morality were offended by Bennett's exploitation of Helen Jewett and urged people not to buy the paper, or any other paper like it.

Pulitzer and Hearst

These efforts to mute the penny press failed miserably. From the 1830s to the 1860s the circulation of newspapers soared. The invention of the telegraph in 1837 was the most important reason. With the telegraph, events from great distances were available instantly, making a good story anywhere in the vast country fair game for editors. The stories themselves often had no immediate relevance to readers, other than as "human interest" stories of murder, lust, and scandal. Newspapers ran telegraph dispatches solely for their power to entertain, to titillate, and to shock.

THE SENSATIONALISTIC NEWSPAPERS THAT CAME INTO PRINT AFTER THE CIVIL WAR THRIVED ON NEWS SUCH AS THE MYSTERIOUS SINKING OF THE *MAINE*, TRUMPETED IN HUGE TYPE IN THIS MULTICOLUMNED HEAD-LINE IN THE FEBRUARY 17, 1898, ISSUE OF THE *NEW YORK WORLD*.

Political persuasion became a secondary concern. Political parties lost their hold on newspapers when advertising revenue, paid circulation, and street sales replaced their sponsorship. The circulation of newspapers rose 400 percent between 1870 and 1900, while the population rose 95 percent. Mechanical invention played an important role in this trend. Joseph Pulitzer's *New York World* introduced the multicolumn headline and the right-hand lead, as well as graphic pictures, colored ink, and cartoons. The "scoop" and the exclusive story became the holy grails of newspaper reporters, who sought to be the first in print with stories meant to shock and surprise. Reporters became cynical about politics, and audiences more wary of printed information. In 1895, E. L. Godkin wrote in the *Nation*: "by the time the young journalist reaches his place he is apt, in good truth, to look on the world as a stage, and the men and women on it as bad actors, and humanity itself, with all its hopes and fears, as simple 'copy'."

The undisputed newspaper king of the era was William Randolph Hearst, who bought the *New York Journal* in 1895. Hearst turned all information into entertainment. The news of the day served as fodder for his reporters' tall tales and, if necessary, he simply invented news on his own to make his papers more appealing to the masses. Hearst injected the *Journal* and its reporters into the events as investigators, and claimed credit for solving murders, cracking spy rings, and uncovering graft and bribery.

In 1897, Hearst saw a golden opportunity in the conflict brewing between Spain and the United States over Cuba, a Spanish colony under siege by rebels fighting for independence. Hearst ran scathing editorials attacking Spain, praising the Cuban rebels, and ridiculing the inaction of the United States government. He prayed for war, and sent dozens of reporters to rustle one up. When the artist Frederick Remington, in Hearst's pay as an illustrator, forlornly cabled from Cuba that nothing of interest was occurring, Hearst famously replied "You provide the pictures. . . . I'll provide the war."

The Spanish-American War did break out, and the *Journal* sold newspapers by the millions. But Hearst's career as a public figure and instigator was only beginning. The Hearst empire grew in power and political influence through the early twentieth century. An entire chain of newspapers, at least one in every major city, served as a personal sounding board for Hearst's own views on politics, entertainment, culture, foreign affairs, business, trade, and war. Editors and reporters followed Hearst's very strict guidelines on the approach they were to take with public figures, presidents, movie stars, and business tycoons.

End of the Partisan Press?

Openly partisan newspapers went out of style in the mid-twentieth century. Newspapers such as the *New York Times* and the *Washington Post* began to strive for a more objective presentation of the news. In-depth, "investigative" articles plumbed hidden facts and motivation, without editorial comment. Journalists grew more careful with words and with the use of sources. Opinions were placed on an opinion or editorial page, where writers contributed their slant on news and issues, editorial cartoonists skewered the high and mighty, and readers contributed letters giving their own views.

In the United States, the partisan press survived in the form of tabloid newspapers. Some were major city dailies, such as New York's *Daily News*, a conservative paper with a loyal base of readers. Tabloid weeklies, such as New York's *Village Voice* and the *L.A. Weekly*, catered to liberal views. Some tabloids continued the tradition of

How Journalism Got Yellow

"THE YELLOW KID" COMIC STRIP WAS CRE-ATED IN **1894** AND WAS A GREAT HIT IN THE **"YELLOW"** NEWSPAPERS OF THE DAY.

The phrase "yellow journalism" means reporting that is lurid, sensationalistic, distorted, often false, and designed solely to attract a mass audience. The term originated in the fierce newspaper rivalries of the late nineteenth century, when William Randolph Hearst's *New York Journal* was engaged in a circulation war with Joseph Pulitzer's *New York World*.

One of the star features of the *World* was "The Yellow Kid," a regular cartoon that appeared in the *World*'s Sunday color supplement. In 1896, William Randolph Hearst hired Outcault, and his cartoon, "The Yellow Kid," moved to the *New York Journal*.

At the same time, a favorite issue for Hearst was the immigration of foreigners—especially Asians—into the United States. This "yellow peril," in Hearst's opinion, threatened native American values and culture.

The color yellow came to be associated with inexpensive newspapers, and the loose standards applied by both Hearst and Pulitzer to the reporting in their newspapers came to be generally known as "yellow journalism." In yellow journalism, news media serve as mouthpieces for political organizations, for the personal prejudices of their owners, or simply as profit centers attempting to win the greatest possible audience with sensationalistic stories. During the twentieth century, when newspapers left the realm of public entertainment and claimed more objectivity and professionalism, "yellow journalism" became the worst insult one could express toward anyone running a news organization.

penny-press sensationalism. The *Weekly World News* and the *National Enquirer* sell hard-to-believe stories of alien kidnappings and strange physical deformities, and photographs of movie and television stars in embarrassing situations. Their most common place of sale gave them the name of "supermarket tabloids."

The mainstream press remains openly partisan in Europe. Newspapers in Great Britain and the continent are still easily identified as conservative, liberal, or centrist. Political parties sponsor newspapers and magazines in France, Italy, and other European countries. These newspapers make no claim to objectivity; their readers accept the underlying bias of the headlines and stories. As a result, there is not much point in Europe of accusing the press of unfair bias, either liberal or conservative. A more important issue for readers is simple accuracy, and the facts of a story that are either emphasized or left out.

In the United States, however, media bias remains a hot issue. Writers dissect news reports, carefully analyzing the facts presented and the words used in order to find an unfair slant. Although the media claim objectivity, many observers don't believe these claims (if they did, they would have little to say, and no opinion of their own to express). In the meantime, new avenues of information are opening up, making media bias an ever more complex issue and, in the opinion of some, a problem that will remain prominent as information is produced and consumed in new ways in the twenty-first century.

2

Television and Blogs

The telegraph transformed the newspaper, eliminating distance and creating instant news. In the mid-nineteenth century, telegraphic dispatches dominated newspaper content. Stories of events anywhere in the country could be relayed instantaneously, giving the reading audience the impression of immediacy and, often, national emergency.

Combined with newspaper photographs, which began appearing in the 1890s, telegraphic dispatches also provided a new form of entertainment. The political content of newspapers lessened, giving way to sensational stories of crime, sex, and scandal. Local concerns no longer dominated newspapers. The telegraph dispatch was largely irrelevant to the daily lives of readers, who became information consumers—and a mass audience.

EDWARD R. MURROW (1908–1965) WAS ONE OF THE MOST RESPECTED OF ALL NEWS BROADCASTERS. MANY THOUGHT THAT MURROW'S *SEE IT NOW* PROGRAM ABOUT SENATOR JOSEPH P. MCCARTHY IN MARCH 1954 WAS INSTRUMENTAL IN BRINGING TO AN END WHAT MANY SEE AS MCCARTHY'S SMEAR CAMPAIGN AGAINST PURPORTED ANTI-COMMUNISTS.

Broadcasting

The broadcasting media of radio and television brought more dramatic changes. During the 1920s, the first commercial radio stations began operating. Radio offered entertainment, music, sports, and news at the touch of a dial, directly inside the home. For millions of families, live national broadcasts ended a sense of isolation and distance. Radio also overcame cultural and social divides. A New York city-dweller and an Iowa farmer, northerners and southerners, blacks, whites, and immigrants, heard the same jokes, listened to the same dance bands, and paid attention to the same news bulletins, speeches, and declarations of war.

The advent of commercial television in the 1950s created the modern electronic news media. Television replaced newspapers as the most important source of information, and completely changed how this information was delivered and received. Many early newscasters, such as Edward R. Murrow and Walter Cronkite, were experienced print journalists who had begun their careers at big-city newspapers in the 1930s and 1940s. As the medium evolved, however, station managers began paying more attention to looks than experience. Television production was expensive, and the networks needed a constant stream of advertising money to stay in business. The only way to guarantee this money was to attract, and hold, a huge national audience. There were many ways to accomplish this. The news was given by readers who appeared attractive or trustworthy, or both, but who had no particular expertise in the fields or events they described. News stories, most lasting less than a minute, appeared as narrated images: interviews, film clips, and live action. Stories ran in rapid succession, one following the next, in a format that allowed very little time for background or analysis. Information became fragmented and distorted. Presentation was geared toward entertainment and toward keeping the reader glued to the screen with compelling images.

Moving images and the "talking heads" of news

broadcasts gave the viewer a sense of immediacy and intimacy. Complex ideas and arguments were lost in favor of teasing intros, very brief summaries, and sound bites— short and memorable phrases used to summarize an event or idea. A reading public could study the complex nuances of public policy. But television served best as an entertainment medium, an evening diversion. Electronic images do not stimulate the work of learning, that is, reasoning, argument, or questioning. They create passive watching and little critical thinking.

Television also had an effect on the way people acted and thought. Many critics saw a society of people passively sitting before a glowing screen, and losing their power to analyze and think. In his book *Amusing Ourselves to Death*, Neil Postman wrote "print . . . gave priority to the objective, rational use of the mind. . . . As the influence of print wanes, the content of politics, religion, education, and anything else that comprises public business must change and be recast in terms that are most suitable to television."

The Effect of Television on Politics

Television became the dominant form of public entertainment and a vital aspect of culture and politics. American politicians had to accommodate their ideas to it. They distilled their positions down to essential sound bites, in the manner of television advertising. They also made sure to look good, an important lesson drawn from the first televised debates between presidential contenders. In September and October 1960, Democrat John F. Kennedy and Republican Richard M. Nixon traded ideas and opinions through four debates, but the impression made in the first debate lingered longest. Recovering from a hospital stay, Nixon looked pale and thin, and the shadow of a beard gave his face a nervous and dark appearance. Kennedy, by contrast, looked tan, fit, and confident. Television viewers were swayed to Kennedy's side, while those who listened to the debate on the radio and couldn't see the candidates were more impressed by Nixon's words and reasoning, and felt he had won the debate.

From this point forward, politicians took great care of their image, trying to appear to be trustworthy, comforting, familiar, and physically fit. They trimmed their messages to make them as easy as possible to understand—like the simple plot of a movie or television show. Political advertising, not stump speeches or position papers or public debate, became the most important aspect of political campaigns. Opposing candidates came up with slogans to sell themselves to the voters, just as auto makers and cereal makers came up with slogans to sell their products.

The fragmented, rapid-fire delivery of television news drew viewers directly into the story in a way that a newspaper or a radio broadcast never could. In the meantime, in this first era of television news, the country was going through social turmoil. The 1960s was the time of the civil rights movement, the Vietnam War, campus demonstrations, and urban race riots. Many young people were experimenting with drugs and new lifestyles that defied convention. A more conservative establishment opposed these changes and saw in them a drastic cultural decline. The Vietnam War divided the country in two: supporters and opponents, and by extension, conservatives and liberals. Television magnified these events, bringing the war and domestic trouble home on the nightly news. As the debate over the war and other issues heated up, both sides pointed to the images and to coverage in the media, and both sides saw rampant bias.

A New Information Medium: Weblogs

In the fall of 2004, during the heat of a closely run presidential campaign, President George W. Bush and challenger John Kerry were under the media microscope. Rumors swirled around the candidates, and campaign aides were busy spinning every story that reached TV networks and newspaper front pages. In the midst of the contest, television viewers witnessed something rare in broadcast journalism: the on-air retraction of a news story.

The story broke on *60 Minutes II*, a television "news magazine" that usually features stories for twenty minutes each in the hour it has to run. In this case, it gave the program a full hour. The broadcast began with the release of four memos it said had been written by Lieutenant Colonel Jerry Killian, a National Guard officer. The documents showed that President Bush had received favored treatment during his time in the Texas Air National Guard. The memos were given by Bill Burkett, a former National Guardsman, to Mary Mapes, a producer for *60 Minutes II*.

A storm erupted even before the show went off the air. Bush supporters accused Burkett and Mapes of using forged documents to discredit the president. They believed that Bush's political enemies had deliberately falsified the documents. They pointed out the modern typography used in the documents—a look of computer-generated text that did not exist in the 1960s, when the memos were supposed to have been written. They pointed out military terminology that was anachronistic (that is, not in use at the time).

CBS News set up a commission to investigate. Its

conclusion was that the network was guilty of sloppy reporting. Dan Rather, head anchor of the CBS Evening News, went on the air to offer an explanation and an apology. The *60 Minutes II* producer who created the story was fired. And the political discredit was minimal for President Bush, as the president was reelected over Democratic candidate Kerry in November.

The "Memogate" scandal, unlike Watergate, did not unfold in the pages of a newspaper. Instead, it caught fire in an unusual medium, a chaotic field of information and debate: the Internet weblog. And it introduced a new concept that promises to change information delivery in a permanent manner: open source media.

The Gulf War and the Blogs

Just as the first Gulf War of 1991 made CNN the most prominent news network on the planet, the second Gulf War introduced the Internet weblog, or "blog." Blogs had not been seen before.

Weblogs are online journals. They arise from the new technology made available to ordinary people through the Internet. In the 1970s, the Internet was only available to the military and to large universities. It served its first subscribers most usefully as an electronic mailbox. Messages could be posted, read, and replied to, with the original posts and replies recorded in a long text document.

Later Internet systems, including Usenet, gave people the ability to create electronic bulletin boards. Professionals could discuss new aspects of their fields. Collectors and hobbyists could share information. Teachers and students could post lessons, reading assignments, and homework. The Usenet groups were particularly useful to software engineers. But anyone with a particular interest, or just an interest in communicating, could make contact with someone else, either across town or on the other side of the planet.

Contact on the Internet could be anonymous, and intensely personal. The Internet did not filter opinion through a public medium such as radio or television, where editors held sway over content, where advertisers did not want to upset the audience, and where federal law banned inflammatory rhetoric and obscenity. On the Internet, ordinary people could give vent to emotions and thoughts that would never be experienced in the traditional media. They didn't have to support their views with evidence, account for contrary opinions, apologize for inaccuracies, watch their language, or remain polite. Politics, in particular, seemed to give rise to extreme words on both sides of the opinion spectrum. The anonymity of the Internet encouraged these extreme views and discouraged conciliation.

New War, New Media

In 1997, Jorn Barger coined "weblog," a word that later became "blog." In 1999, Blogger, software designed for creating weblogs, appeared on the market. With Blogger and other software that followed, users not trained in Web programming could easily set up their own weblogs. They could allow others to post replies, or create new "threads," or topics of discussion, that could head in any direction. The blogger could attract new users by sending out updates and invitations. Users could be updated by e-mail whenever a new reply was posted to these threads.

In the matter of politics and current events, the weblog came into its own during the second Gulf War, which began in the spring of 2003. Those supporting and those opposing the war gave free rein to their opinions. Many U.S. soldiers in Iraq created weblogs ("milblogs") to convey their fear and frustration, as well as the pride they took in their mission. Iraqis also set up weblogs to express their own, sometimes very critical, opinions about the war.

One Iraqi blogger, using the pen name Aunt Najma, used Blogger software to set up a weblog in June 2004. Her Web site, "A Star from Mosul," offers a short biography, entries describing her life in the northern city of Mosul, links to other blogs created by her relatives, and an archive. Aunt Najma proudly displays two badges of honor, her Honorable Mention by the Brass Crescent Awards, given to the best Iraqi bloggers, and her Finalist win in the 2004 Weblog Awards.

Like many blogs created in Iraq, Aunt Najma's mixes politics and personal life, ordinary happenings and the terrors of war. She began the blog with a post telling of a trip to the dentist, and ending with:

> he [the dentist] was talking to my mother about an explosion that happened a day ago, near the clinic, all the patients ran to their houses, he was lucky the windows were opened because otherwise they would definitely break because of the pressure. . . . Who knows maybe the situation will get better now, we have a new government now, at least there's no explosions, so far :-) . . . I won't talk about politics, you can find it everywhere. I have too much things to do today, all on the internet.

Bloggers dealing with the Iraq war also used their Web sites to post information, gleaned from any source they could find, to support their positions on the war. Ordinary standards of journalism didn't apply. Their sources could be important people in the government, the military, or a large corporation. On the other hand, a friend or a relative could use the weblog to spread a rumor or a false story. These sources could be named, faked, or anonymous. No editor or producer worried about accuracy, or dealt with contrary evidence and public criticism. Sources never needed to be checked out, and retractions never had to be made.

The Blogs and Trent Lott

As the second Gulf War unfolded under this attention, politics in the United States also attracted partisan opinion in the weblog medium. Bloggers found they could fuel controversies and keep scandal alive long after the "mainstream media" had dropped one story for the next one.

One of the first politicians to feel the heat from weblogs was Trent Lott, a Republican senator from Mississippi and, since 1996, the Senate Majority Leader. Like many politicians, Lott was always very careful about what he said in the Senate and especially careful when speaking to reporters. But at banquets, fund-raising dinners, and other informal functions, he was less careful. Although comments made at such occasions are still fair game for any reporters present, the media usually gives them less coverage than official speeches.

At one such dinner in December 2002, Lott was honoring South Carolina Senator Strom Thurmond at Thurmond's one-hundredth birthday celebration. Lott thought he would do little harm to himself or anyone else with the following remark:

> **I want to say this about my state: When Strom Thurmond ran for president, we voted for him. We're proud of it. And if the rest of the country had followed our lead, we wouldn't have had all these problems over all these years.**

SENATOR TRENT LOTT'S CAREER BEGAN TO UNRAVEL WHEN REMARKS HE MADE AT SENATOR STROM THURMOND'S ONE-HUNDREDTH BIRTHDAY WERE WIDELY DISSEMINATED ON A WEBLOG AND THEN PICKED UP BY THE MAINSTREAM MEDIA.

Lott had made a very similar remark twenty-five years earlier, when he was still a young and inexperienced member of the House of Representatives from Mississippi. His comment, made during a campaign speech in support of Ronald Reagan, attracted little notice and no scandal. But in 2003, things were different, and so was the public information media.

Bloggers picked up Lott's remarks and turned them into a full-fledged embarassment for the senator. Weblogs researched previous speeches made by Lott, and delved into Strom Thurmond's history as a segregationist and a white supremacist. In the "blogosphere," Lott was accused of being sympathetic to these positions, which Thurmond himself had long abandoned. Previous speeches of Lott's were posted online to demonstrate this. Television and newspapers used this information to keep the story alive and the pressure on Lott.

Lott apologized for his remarks, calling them a "poor choice of words." His Republican ally, President George W. Bush, harshly and publicly criticized the remarks—a rare action for a president to take against a powerful Senate leader from his own party. Despite Lott's apology, the damage had been done. Eventually, he resigned his position as Senate Majority Leader, and any hopes he had of running for higher office came to an abrupt end.

Open Sources

The debunking of the National Guard memos concerning President Bush, and the poor word choices of Senator Lott, introduced a new concept in information media: the blogstorm. This heavy media turbulence occurs when partisan bloggers get hold of a news story and attempt to transform it into a national news event. Bloggers from all parts of the political spectrum weigh in with opinions and rumors, keeping the controversy alive by lending it a new twist, turn, or suggestion each day. The blogstorm feeds on itself, and then spins off into mainstream media, where the same information is published or broadcast to an even wider audience.

Blogstorms occur because, on the Internet or in broadcasting, voices of moderation can be easily out-shouted by extremists, who pitch their views with a fervor that casual readers find more entertaining. News stories turn into scandals, and then into show business, with the loudest voices catching the best ratings and biggest audiences. Those who see weblogs as the wave of the future hail the new "open source" media, in which anyone and everyone can make a contribution. Most bloggers aren't motivated by money, as are large media companies. The vast majority are produced at the personal expense of those who wish simply to express their opinion. They don't sell ad space or subscriptions, and don't have to answer to corporate bosses concerned with profit. In this way, advocates argue, blogs are a more democratic medium, in which new voices are heard, and the filter of big-business media outlets is swept aside for a version of the story much closer to the truth.

Another perspective on weblogs: the weblog gains fame and attention from distortion and scandal. Something very different happens to the "mainstream media" in which professional journalists, who are expected to check and double-check their sources, are tarred with the black brush of bias and favoritism. In the words of Corey Pein in the *Columbia Journalism Review*: "CBS couldn't prove the authenticity of the documents in its story, and look at the results. Rather has announced his resignation under a cloud and his aggressive news division is tarnished. And the coverage of Memogate effectively killed the story of Bush's Guard years. Those who kept asking questions found themselves counted among the journalistic fringe."

Television

Pro

- Television makes news immediate, allowing the audience to receive information instantaneously, from anywhere in the world.
- Television allows viewers to see, up close, the actors in important current events.
- Television brings home wars, natural disasters, plagues, and famine, which in turn spurs on people and organizations to counter these problems.
- Television is an effective medium for the investigation of criminal behavior. Reporters can interview victims, suspects, witnesses, police, and lawyers; give important background information; follow trials day by day; and summarize important points of law.

Con

- Television trivializes politics and turns the entire political process into lightweight entertainment.
- Television networks seek to attract and hold a large audience, in order to earn more money from advertising (advertising rates are based on the size of the audience). To hold an audience, television cuts quickly from one subject to the next, emphasizing the visual aspects of a story. By presenting information in this fragmented, hurried manner, television affects people's ability to pay attention, and to think about and comprehend serious issues.

• Powerful media companies and well-funded politicians have learned to use television to sway public opinion in their favor.

• The twenty-four-hour television "news cycle" puts reporters under tremendous pressure and forces them to cut corners in gathering news. The result is speculation, reliance on rumors (especially those sent out over weblogs and the Internet), unconfirmed information, and outright falsehood passed off as fact.

Weblogs

Pro

• Weblogs give a forum to individuals who would never reach the mainstream media with their knowledge, experiences, and opinions.

• The "democratizing" of information takes it out of the hands of large, profit-driven companies.

• Weblogs allow the public to debate issues outside the entertainment medium of television.

Con

• The Internet has never been known for its truthfulness and accuracy. False information can move a lot faster on the Web than a true story that has been checked and verified by the mainstream media.

• Weblogs have become a soapbox for extremists and ranters.

• The sheer number buries any meaningful dialogue in a mass of trivial verbiage.

Bias and Perception

In theory, an informed public is best able to make wise decisions about public policy. The job of the media is to present information. Ideally, personal and political bias is kept out of the presentation of news. In the real world, bias is present in many forms: in language used, in the presentation of the story, in the quotes used from interviews, and in background information. Each aspect means a choice on the part of the reporter. No matter how hard a reporter tries to be completely objective, he or she must choose words, context, and emphasis. In these details a thorough critic can always find bias of some kind.

Few people make the claim that unbiased media is a reality. But the origins of the bias, according to the two sides of the debate, lie in very different directions. Those who believe the media is biased toward the conservative point of view see reports conforming to formulas set down by their bosses and the wealthy corporations that employ them. Those who believe the media have a liberal bias think reporters have left-wing political leanings that creep into their presentation of the news. Those who believe this think that these reporters see left-wing positions as moderate and reasonable, and they tend to support Democratic candidates. In addition, these reporters and editors make up an elite: "Now, leading journalists are courted by politicians, studied by scholars and known to millions through their bylines and televised images," Brent Baker and Brent Bozell comment in *And That's the Way It Isn't*. "In short, the needs of a society increasingly hungry for information have contributed to the rise of a national news network—the new media elite."

Conservatives also point out that big media companies are concentrated on the east and west coasts, in New York and Hollywood. As a result, the ethos of these regions— predominantly liberal—and of urban America dominates media. The more conservative heart of the country, and its outlooks and concerns, are ignored.

Follow the Leader

Media superpowers have dominated information for many decades. The production of news is expensive, and only large companies can make the needed investment in equipment, licenses, property, and employees. To increase their income, large media companies always seek to buy smaller ones. The result is fewer media companies, and more conformity in the way news is presented. It has been a long time since the invention of the telegraph, and the amount of information at hand is greater than it has ever been. But all reporters, both print and electronic, rely largely on only a few sources of information: the three television networks, the major cable networks, the Associated Press, Reuters, and United Press International wire services, and a few daily newspapers, including the *New York Times*, the *Washington Post*, the *Los Angeles Times*, and the *Wall Street Journal*.

This game of follow-the-leader makes news reporting conform to a very narrow range of stories. Smaller newspapers don't have the money to pay a large staff of reporters, or set up bureaus in distant cities and countries. They run most of their front-page stories verbatim from these media superpowers. Although they may assign a reporter to cover local reaction to that story, they do no investigation of their own on national or international events.

All over the United States, people are reading identical news reports, reprinted most often from the *New York Times* or the *Washington Post*. Opinion writers "brand" themselves, like fast-food chains or cars, by following a reliably liberal or conservative viewpoint, always slanting the information their way and giving a positive "spin" to their own causes and the politicians they support. Editors don't want to anger their audience by surprising them with stories outside the predictable mainstream, and look to circulation or audience size, and advertising sales, as the measure of their success.

Because media outlets are profit-driven corporations, the selling of advertising also casts a long shadow over what can be presented as information. Advertisers can generate influence over the way news is handled by threatening to end their sponsorship. In fear of this, editors may kill stories casting an unfavorable light on the advertisers. In some cases, large corporations are outright owners of important media outlets. General Electric, for example, a large industrial corporation, owns both MSNBC and NBC. Disney, the largest entertainment company in the United States, owns the ABC television network. The chances of these networks running with any news story that hurts their corporate parents is slim, and as a result the public can be cheated out of vital information.

The Dominant Left

In general, conservatives don't mind large companies owning media outlets. They object, instead, to what they see as a natural liberal bias among employees, editors, and reporters. They also see a left-wing bias at the wealthiest, most prominent media companies. Bernard Goldberg, a critic of liberal bias, comments, "The problem is that so

PRESIDENT GEORGE W. BUSH IS SHOWN CARRYING BERNARD GOLDBERG'S BOOK, *BIAS*—WHICH CLAIMS THE MEDIA IS PREJUDICED TOWARD THE LIBERAL POINT OF VIEW—AS HE LEAVES FOR A TRIP TO PORTLAND, MAINE, ON JANUARY 25, 2002.

many TV journalists simply don't know what to think about certain issues until the *New York Times* and the *Washington Post* tell them what to think. Those big, important newspapers set the agenda that network news people follow."

Goldberg had an insider's view of the problem. He joined CBS News in 1972 and became a national correspondent for the network in 1981. In the mid-1990s, Goldberg grew increasingly unhappy with what he saw as liberal bias among colleagues and bosses at the network. He clashed with his bosses over the treatment of stories on the evening news and on weekly television feature news shows such as *60 Minutes*. On February 13, 1996, he went public with his grievance in the editorial pages of the *Wall Street Journal*. Goldberg described an unfair treatment of the "flat tax," an idea proposed by conservative presidential candidate Steve Forbes. In 2002, Goldberg resigned from CBS, and two years later he published *Bias*, a book slamming CBS and the media in general for what he saw as a relentless liberal slant on the news.

Goldberg's book made a splash with its claims of bias and its assertion that journalists and liberals simply aren't everyday Americans. *Bias* stated that:

> one of the biggest problems in big-time journalism: its elites are hopelessly out of touch with everyday Americans. Their friends are liberals, just as they are. They share the same values. Almost all of them think the same way on the big social issues of our time: abortion, gun control, feminism, gay rights, the environment, school prayer. After a while they start to believe that all civilized people think the same way they and their friends do. That's why they don't simply disagree with conservatives. They see them as morally deficient.

Unhappy with what he perceived as liberal bias—and seeing a vast potential audience among conservatives—Rupert Murdoch created the Fox News Channel. Murdoch owned a global media company and, in the style of William Randolph Hearst, had used sensationalism and conservative politics to build the News Corporation, a global chain of newspapers and satellite cable stations. Launched in New York in 1996, Fox News claimed to have a fair and balanced point of view, according to its slogan, "We report, you decide." Murdoch hired Roger Ailes to run the network, which soon was competing head-to-head with CNN. Before he developed Fox News, Ailes had served the Republican Party and conservative causes for years as a political adviser and media consultant. With Fox News, he went straight from politics to the media—claiming for the first time in his career to offer a balanced presentation of the issues.

Critics of Fox don't believe him, pointing out a consistent conservative bias in Fox's news broadcasts and opinion shows. Conservatives see on Fox a balanced presentation, as well as an answer to the liberal slant on CNN and other networks. They also point out Fox's high ratings—in a short time, Fox became as popular with the U.S. television audience as CNN. At the very least, in this view, Fox has found a very large market for its content, which in the media world is the final measure of success.

Laziness

A larger problem than political bias—basic human laziness—affects the presentation of news. The twenty-four-hour "news cycle" of constant, breaking stories puts reporters under heavy deadline pressure. They are expected to come up with interesting news and quotes on a daily basis. When reporting a story, they may take an easy route to the deadline by using information already published or broadcast by a rival. They may turn to familiar sources whom they can rely on to provide a quote that supports their point of view. They can also use sources without identifying them. These "anonymous" sources are a valuable tool of all reporters, who jealously guard them, knowing that to reveal names may end up permanently costing them valuable cooperation.

Reporters also may rely on press agents, publicists, official spokesmen, and printed press releases that are used by government agencies, companies, and organizations to present their side of the facts and the story. These official sources need good publicity. The best way to create this publicity, and positive "spin" for those they represent, is to get a positive story into print or on the television news. In the words of Martin Lee and Norman Solomon in *Unreliable Sources*:

> **High-level journalists and high-placed sources need each other. Whatever the tensions, cooperation is routine. . . . Various studies bear out this assertion. For example, a sampling of 2,850 articles in the *New York Times* and the *Washington Post* found 78 percent to be primarily based on the words of public officials. The same sources dominate TV news.**

In 2003, Judith Miller, an experienced reporter for the *New York Times*, wrote several articles on the building of weapons of mass destruction (WMDs)—nuclear, chemical, and biological (germ) weapons—in Saddam Hussein's Iraq. In her reporting, Miller relied on

NEW YORK TIMES REPORTER JUDITH MILLER WAS JAILED FOR
EIGHTY-FIVE DAYS BECAUSE SHE REFUSED TO REVEAL HER SOURCES
FOR INFORMATION RELATED TO A GOVERNMENT INVESTIGATION OF A
LEAK OF INFORMATION REGARDING VALERIE PLAME, A FORMER
CIA AGENT.

sources—both in and out of the American government—
who wanted to raise public support for a war in Iraq. Several worked at intelligence units within the Pentagon, and
got their information from Ahmad Chalabi, an Iraqi exile
whom the Bush administration intended to support as a
new leader in post-war Iraq. In this way, Miller and the
Times served the purpose not of providing unbiased information to the public, but of providing a public relations
service to the administration and to an individual who
had political ambitions in Iraq. After the invasion of Iraq,
the U.S. military searched in vain for Iraq's WMD arsenal,
while questions about his administration's case for war,
and its true motivations, baffled and angered the president.

Russell Baker, in an article written in the *Nation*, blames
the Miller WMD-nonstory on the media star system:

> **Out of the hundreds of thousands of jour-
> nalists in America, just a handful enter the
> firmament of media stars, and Miller is one
> of them. . . . Because reporters at these
> levels get unparalleled access to high-level
> sources, they are uniquely positioned to
> publish information that powerfully impacts
> government policy, public perceptions, and
> even life on earth. By the same token, high-
> level sources use these journalists to selec-
> tively make public material that is helpful to
> their agenda.**

Anonymous sources can be useful to reporters as well as
the public. If someone is assured of keeping his or her name
out of the press, for example, then it will be easier to reveal
the misconduct of a public official. The frequent use of anonymous sources for information also makes journalists depend-
ent. Using the staffer of a member of Congress as a source,
for example, a reporter comes to depend on the member of

Edward R. Murrow

The most respected journalist in U.S. television history, Edward R. Murrow, was famous for his objectivity and honesty. Murrow began his broadcast career as a radio reporter, sending home gripping live reports from England during World War II. In the 1950s, his *See it Now* weekly news program pioneered the format still used by *60 Minutes* and other television magazines. The first installment of *See it Now* was also the first broadcast to include live reports from the east and west coasts of the United States.

Murrow's most renowned TV reporting dealt with Senator Joseph McCarthy and the anti-Communist hysteria of the mid–1950s. The "Red Scare" had whipped the country into a frenzy of paranoia; thousands of people in all walks of life came under suspicion as Communist sympathizers. Murrow spent several months investigating McCarthy's accusations of Communist Party membership on the part of government officials and military officers.

On March 9, 1954, *See it Now* presented a detailed investigation of McCarthy himself. Murrow purposefully made McCarthy look devious and hypocritical by broadcasting contradictory statements from the senator's own speeches. In the first minutes of the program, Murrow quoted McCarthy as saying, "The American people realize this cannot be made a fight between America's two great political parties," then quoted the Republican senator later calling the Democrats treasonous: "The hard fact is that those who wear the label Democrat . . . wear it with the stain of historic betrayal." Murrow also pointed out McCarthy's attempt to smear Reed Harris, a member of the U.S. Department of State. In a Senate hearing, McCarthy badgered Harris about a book he had written twenty years earlier, about the fact that he had been suspended from Columbia University, and that he had been defended by a lawyer from the American Civil Liberties Union (ACLU)—in McCarthy's view, a subversive, Communist-front organization.

Murrow commented on the program, "We proclaim ourselves, as indeed we are, the defenders of freedom, wherever it continues to exist in the world, but we cannot defend freedom abroad by deserting it at home." Murrow's eloquence, and his use of well-researched facts and public statements, presented a devastating case against McCarthy, a case largely free of personal political bias. The *See it Now* program exposed McCarthy's flaws much more effectively than any political leader could, and played a big role in McCarthy's eventual fall from power.

Congress. In order to maintain access to the source, the reporter probably will avoid writing anything negative about him or her. In turn, the source uses the reporter as a way of leaking information damaging to his or her enemies. This relationship usually slants news the source's way.

The use of official sources introduces bias of its own. Only the official, approved version of events is presented to the public. Dissent against this version is faint, sometimes ignored altogether. The public is poorly served with half a story, and makes poorly informed decisions about important events. Powers-that-be are supported in their mismanagement of public affairs, and come to realize that poor judgment and incompetence have no consequences.

The problems of corporate control, anonymous sources, and political bias, in the view of many, is less important than the problems of the television medium. Neil Postman sees important issues being trivialized into evening entertainment: "the television news show entertains but does not inform . . . we are losing our sense of what it means to be well informed." Postman believes "television has achieved the power to define the form in which news must come, and it has also defined how we shall respond to it. In presenting news to us packaged as vaudeville, television induces other media to do the same."

Which Is It?

A Liberal Media

- **Most reporters are politically liberal and so give a liberal slant to stories they report.**
- **The elite media moguls in New York and California favor liberal causes and politicians, while ignoring the interests of more conservative people of the heartland.**

A Conservative Media

- The big media companies are owned and operated by conservative individuals and corporations, more interested in making money than in providing balanced coverage or in including truly liberal points of view.
- The use of government-approved information sources, press releases, and official speeches favors the conservative powers-that-be.
- Advertising exerts too much power over the content of news stories, making editors reluctant to rock the boat over social and environmental issues.

4

Watergate

The modern media thrive on scandal. The misbehavior of famous people and politicians has become the star attraction in the information mix. But the media have not always worried about such misbehavior. Before the turn of the twentieth century, political leaders were largely immune from personal scandal. Although their policies and public actions often came under attack, their private lives and professional crimes held little interest for newspaper editors.

The "Progressive" era in journalism changed all that. In the early twentieth century, reporters became investigators. Journalists attacked big business for its unlawful monopolies, for poor working conditions, and for bribery. Politicians came under the microscope for election crimes—buying votes and intimidating voters—and for graft (accepting money and favors for their votes as lawmakers). Ida Tarbell wrote about the huge Standard Oil trust in *McClure's* magazine; Lincoln Steffens uncovered the corruption of "Boss Tweed" and the Tammany Hall political machine in New York City. Jacob Riis, Upton Sinclair, and John Spargo wrote about child labor, sweatshops, and the desperate lives of ordinary workers in big city factories, mills, and slaughterhouses.

President Theodore Roosevelt had a name for these investigations: "muckraking." As a Progressive politician, Roosevelt heartily approved of these stories. He wanted a reform of bad business practices and political corruption, and saw the press as his ally in this work. But later in the century, President Richard Nixon took a different view of investigative journalism. In his view, the press was simply out to get him. He saw scandalmongering as a hallmark of the media's bias against him. In the end, his worst fears were realized.

The Watergate Break-In

The evening of June 17, 1972, seemed quiet and uneventful at the Watergate Hotel in downtown Washington, D.C. Frank Wills, the night security guard, was making his rounds in the hallways and stairwells of the hotel. Normally, Wills simply checked the doors to make sure locks were working properly. At a door to the parking garage, Wills found a piece of duct tape holding the door open—and thought it had been put there by a cleaning crew. When he returned, however, the tape had been replaced. Wills called in the police, who discovered five men burglarizing the headquarters of the Democratic National Committee. The events that followed would topple a president and, in the process, transform the American media.

A *Washington Post* reporter, Bob Woodward, was present at the arraignment of James McCord, one of the Watergate burglars. In the police investigation of the burglary, it was discovered that McCord had once worked for the Committee to Re-elect the President, the organization that was part of President Richard Nixon's 1972 campaign. McCord also happened to have the telephone number of a Nixon White House aide, E. Howard Hunt, written down in one of his notebooks.

At his arraignment, McCord claimed to be an agent of the Central Intelligence Agency. The district attorney of Washington, D.C., discovered that he was receiving payments from the Committee to Re-elect the President. The case drew the interest of editors at the *Washington Post*. Woodward and Carl Bernstein spent months tracking the case through the courts, interviewing sources, developing leads, and untangling a web of connections leading back to the White House. They also made contact with a highly placed government official who arranged to meet them in an underground parking garage on the outskirts of Washington, D.C. Nicknamed "Deep Throat," the source tipped them off to various illegal activities ordered by the Nixon White House.

G. GORDON LIDDY, AIDE TO PRESIDENT RICHARD M. NIXON, WALKS OUT OF THE U.S. DISTRICT COURT AFTER PLEADING NOT GUILTY TO CHARGES OF BREAKING INTO DEMOCRATIC NATIONAL HEADQUARTERS AT THE WATERGATE HOTEL. HE WAS LATER CONVICTED OF CONSPIRACY, BURGLARY, AND WIRETAPPING, AND SERVED A PRISON TERM.

In their articles, Woodward and Bernstein revealed that the Watergate burglary and numerous other "dirty tricks" had been ordered by the Committee to Re-elect the President, by E. Howard Hunt, and by another Nixon aide, G. Gordon Liddy. President Nixon, who had always seen the news media as his enemy, declared war on the *Post* and its reporters. David Brock comments: "Journalists dominated the enemies list that Nixon asked his White House counsel, John Dean, to draw up. The telephones of several reporters were wiretapped by the government. . . . During Watergate, Nixon schemed to challenge the *Washington Post's* broadcast licenses . . ."

In January 1973, Hunt, Liddy, and the Watergate burglars went on trial. All were convicted of conspiracy, burglary, and wiretapping. The convictions did not end the Watergate story. A Senate committee, under Senator Sam Ervin, began its own investigation. The Watergate committee subpoenaed members of the White House to testify. Through the summer of 1973, the Senate Watergate committee heard dozens of high-level witnesses testify—on live, national television. The Watergate hearings ran from morning till late afternoon, every business day, and drew a massive audience.

On July 13, the committee discovered that Nixon had taped every conversation he held with aides in the Oval Office. When the Senate committee subpoenaed these tapes, Nixon refused to supply them. Eventually, the White House released transcripts of the tapes to the committee—with a crucial eighteen-minute section deliberately erased. In July 1974, the Supreme Court ordered the tapes released. Soon afterward, the House of Representatives passed three articles of impeachment, which, if supported by a full vote of Congress, would have forced Nixon to leave office.

Before that could happen, on August 8, 1974, Nixon resigned. Vice President Gerald Ford then succeeded Nixon, and on September 8 issued a full pardon for the former president. The pardon protected Nixon from any prosecution for his part in the Watergate burglary and cover-up.

In the spring of 2005, "Deep Throat" came forward in an article for *Vanity Fair* magazine. He was W. Mark Felt, the second-in-command at the Federal Bureau of Investigation during the Watergate investigation. Felt himself was involved in the investigation, and believed that the president was illegally interfering with the FBI and trying to cover up the scandal. Felt's actions still stirred up bitter debate more than thirty years later. Nixon's supporters and former aides came forward to condemn Felt for his betrayal of the president's confidence and his leaking of sensitive and classified information. "There's nothing heroic about breaking faith with your people, breaking the law, sneaking around in garages, putting stuff from an investigation out to a Nixon-hating *Washington Post*," said Pat Buchanan, a former Nixon aide. Others hailed him as a hero, praising his role in uncovering corruption at the very top.

Watergate and the Media

News media history can be divided into "before" and "after" Watergate. The press in the years before Watergate had kept mainly to public issues such as foreign affairs, economic policy, election reporting, and the ups and downs of political parties. After Watergate, the press saw its role in a different light. In *Who Will Tell the People*, William Greider comments that "Watergate . . . became a statement about political power: a thunder-and-lightning announcement that the news media had claimed a new place among the governing elites."

The investigation of Watergate by Woodward, Bernstein, and the *Washington Post* created a model for reporters across the country. Newspapers and broadcast outlets sought out public scandal of any type—political

On May 31, 2005, former FBI deputy director Mark Felt and his daughter Joan Felt spoke to reporters outside his home in Santa Rosa, California, after he had revealed himself to be the long-protected "Deep Throat."

or personal—an attempt to grab headlines and sell newspapers. In this new environment, the private problems of public figures became fair game. "The *Post*'s Watergate triumph . . . spawned a thousand imitators and changed political relationships everywhere," Greider notes. The executive branch of government lost much of its power and respect, while the press drew praise and widespread admiration.

Just a few months after the resignation of President Nixon, Congressman Wilbur Mills was involved in a drunken driving incident. Before Watergate, the incident would have probably been ignored. Twentieth-century newspaper editors saw themselves as progressing past the innuendo and rumor of the yellow-journalism era, and usually glossed over the personal issues of politicians, such as drunkenness, womanizing, gambling, or ill health. This time the press was all over the story, and Mills suffered the same end as Nixon—forced to resign his office. In the 1980s, the media took up the Iran-Contra scandal, revealing that Ronald Reagan's administration was running a secret arms deal with Iran in an attempt to free American hostages in the Middle East. And the 1990s brought a series of press scandals for President Bill Clinton. The investigations began soon after Clinton took office and continued until his final days. One story, about his sexual affair with a young White House intern, eventually led to his impeachment by Congress. Clinton barely survived a vote to impeach him on charges of perjury and obstruction of justice.

Investigative journalism doesn't always get favorable reviews. Some believe that newspapers and broadcast media play up scandal on purpose. "Investigation" becomes "speculation," as journalists seek the Watergate-style fame of Woodward and Bernstein, and editors seek juicy headlines for the sake of selling copies. In the opinion of many, the taste for scandal makes media outlets biased, as the

The Nattering Nabobs

From the beginning of his first term as president in 1969, the media was a serious problem for President Richard Nixon. Since his defeat in the 1960 election, which he blamed on a poor television image, Nixon had always seen the media as his adversary. He constantly complained about the negative treatment his policies, and particularly the war in Vietnam, received in newspapers and on television. His vice president, Spiro Agnew, was a staunch defender of the war and an even harsher critic of war protestors and, in particular, the media.

At a speech given to the California Republican convention in 1970, Agnew delivered the following opinion on the press: "In the United States today, we have more than our share of the nattering nabobs of negativism. They have formed their own 4-H Club—the hopeless, hysterical hypochondriacs of history." These lines, delivered by Agnew but written by White House speechwriter William Safire, remain the most famous condemnation of press bias by any public official.

Agnew and Nixon would both have good reason to complain about their treatment in the press. Two years later, Nixon's presidency would begin to unravel with the Watergate scandal, an affair covered by hundreds of investigative reporters. And Agnew himself would resign in 1973 under accusations of bribery and tax evasion in his home state of Maryland. Agnew pleaded "no contest" to the charges, which were avidly covered by the press. The Republican fear of the press lingered on in the following generation, when Republican politicians and conservatives in general saw the mainstream American media as their ideological enemy.

press itself seeks to protect its reputation by making scandals appear worse than they really are. Conservatives, in particular, have a problem with the Watergate affair. Many are convinced that Nixon's demise was brought about by a conspiracy among his political opponents in the media. Adrian Woolridge, co-author of *The Right Nation*, points out that "the conservative establishment was very much spawned by the reaction to what happened to Nixon."

Others believe the media plays an important role as a "watchdog." They point to Watergate as a triumph of journalism, an example of the vital role the media play in an open, democratic society. They admire the muckraking abilities of journalists and believe that if the press doesn't uncover corruption in high places, then nobody else will. In this view, conservatives angered by Watergate have, since Nixon's resignation in 1974, eagerly promoted media scandals of their own against Democrats and liberals—in order to even the score.

Investigative Reporting

Pros
   • Investigative reporting uncovers illegal actions of political leaders, helping to keep them honest.
   • The public has a right and a need to know about such misbehavior.
   • The media play an important role that no other institution will.

Cons
   • Scandal is played up for the sake of better sales and circulation.
   • The media are used as a weapon by those seeking to undermine those they oppose politically.
   • Public trust in elected officials is undermined by false stories and innuendo.

Media, Politics, and the (Very) Personal

An information explosion occurred at the end of the twentieth century. The sources of news multiplied manyfold. This strongly affected the way people receive information and how they dealt with the information received.

At one time, most people had only a single source of public information—the daily newspaper. Television introduced national news broadcasts over a small handful of commercial networks. Every evening, around dinnertime, the networks simultaneously broadcast a half-hour of what producers considered the most interesting stories. Often, the stories running on each network were the same, and only the presentation differed.

The networks presented their news with an anchor, who sat at a desk, looked the viewer in the eye, and solemnly read the news. Network anchors were stars, and their familiar faces bred trust in people who watched them, night after night, at the same time.

Cable television started a transformation in the presentation of news. First developed in 1948 in Mahanoy City, Pennsylvania, cable television was a way of bundling several television stations together and delivering them to subscribers via a wire (rather than broadcasting through the air). In 1980, Ted Turner established the Cable News Network, the first all-news network. CNN presented a continuous program of news stories and headlines, with the stories repeated every half-hour and regularly updated. Instead of arriving at a set time every evening, television news became a constant stream, running all day and all night.

The invention of twenty-four-hour news had several important effects. Viewers no longer had to pay very close attention if they wanted to stay informed. Dinnertime or breakfast-time served as well as any other time to get the news. In addition, the twenty-four-hour news program demanded constant newness. Television producers sought out new stories and rushed them to the airwaves, simply for the sake of having something new to present. Many of these stories were trivial and of little national interest; local events made the cable-news headlines and were abruptly dropped the next day for the sake of the next, equally trivial story.

Cable television offered viewers dozens, sometimes hundreds, of channels to replace the three tried-and-true national networks of the past. Viewers had a huge menu of channels to choose from (as well as video cassette players and, later, dvds that could run movies and replace televised programming at any time). The amount of time spent watching any single station fell drastically, while specialized cable stations, such as MTV (music videos) and ESPN (sports) competed for viewers. CNN and other networks had to offer something unique, or uniquely entertaining, to hold viewers at all. As a result, the news became a running picture show, with images selected to shock or titillate, and stories shortened to match an ever-shorter attention span on the part of viewers.

A New Style in the Media

At one time, newspaper stories could be thousands of words long when dealing with a weighty social issue, a political campaign, or a crisis overseas. In the television medium, anchors and reporters had to tell the story in a minute or two. The stories they ran, as a result, lost their weight. While the most important subject in news media remains politics, the style of this coverage changed in the late twentieth century. The personal lives of politicians became fair game for news coverage.

This change occurred slowly. It had not yet occurred by the time of World War II. The subject of President Franklin Roosevelt's polio, which confined him to a wheelchair, was given wide berth by newspaper reporters and photographers. The public never saw him walk and never saw his legs. President John F. Kennedy's personal life and troubles were also off limits. Kennedy engaged in many extramarital affairs as president. But the press never wrote about them.

Then came Watergate and the resignation of President Richard Nixon. A large percentage of the population had taken a personal dislike to Nixon. His mannerisms and way of speaking made him a target of reporters and cartoonists. Nixon seemed suspicious and defensive, as if he had something to hide. The Watergate scandal confirmed this idea in the minds of the public, who witnessed his face and mannerisms each evening, close up, in their living rooms. The intimacy of televised images gave the illusion that he was a member of the family. People took a deep interest in, and formed strong opinions about, Nixon's personality.

The effect of television, and the taste for scandal sparked by Watergate, created very "personal" media journalism. Betty Ford, the wife of President Gerald Ford, Nixon's successor, experienced breast cancer as well as a hard struggle with alcoholism, which were covered thoroughly in newspapers and on television. While at one time these subjects would have been off-limits, the post-Watergate media didn't hesitate to discuss Ms. Ford's problems and treatment. As always, newspapers were seeking high circulation and broadcast outlets high ratings.

The Horse Race

In this new kind of news media, issues took a back seat. Social and economic problems required complex solutions and complex reporting, and this kind of coverage didn't rate highly among the mainstream. The taste for "tabloid" or sensationalistic personal coverage came out strongest during elections. The press focused on the horse race—who was winning and who was losing. Opinion polls ran frequently, showing the voting trends of a very small sample of the population. Colorful election maps were given a prominent place, with each candidate's conquered territory marked in a different, bright color. By the election of 2004, the election map had taken over political debate in the media. "Blue" (liberal) and "red" (conservative) states won by Democrats and Republicans, respectively, became a common metaphor in talking about the political and cultural differences in American society.

The media used rumor and scandal to sell their election coverage to the public. In 1988, this new approach caught up with Democratic presidential candidate Gary Hart. Rumors of his extramarital affairs were covered in the pages of the *New York Times*, a newspaper with wide influence and global circulation. Politicians take coverage in the *Times* very seriously and feel called on to respond to any negative stories in that paper. Hart angrily denied the rumors and threw down this challenge: "Follow me around. I don't care. I'm serious. If anybody wants to put a tail on me, go ahead. They'll be very bored."

The press obliged. A photograph of Gary Hart sitting on a boat, with a woman perched on his knees, appeared in the *National Enquirer*, a tabloid newspaper. The woman in the photograph, Donna Rice, was not Gary Hart's wife, and the name of the boat was *Monkey Business*. Mainstream news outlets could not resist whipping up a scandal. The photograph appeared in newspapers and on television stations all over the country, and Hart's campaign for president abruptly ended.

A Bias for Sex

In the Hart scandal, the media made the personal life of a presidential candidate fair game. Some considered the treatment unfair to Hart. They didn't like the media turning election coverage into a "soap opera," in which reporters speculated on the hidden life of the candidates away from the cameras. Policy issues lost prominence in this new reporting, while the press focused on whether candidates cheated on their wives, or drank too much, or had used drugs while in college.

Others saw very "personal" aspects of their elected leaders as fair game. They didn't want a hidden side to people with big responsibilities. The personal weaknesses of a president, in this view, might have a very real effect on his actions in public. They wanted to know if the people they might vote for were liars, cheaters, or drunkards. They hailed the new and personal coverage of politics—especially if it benefited the side they supported.

The scandal didn't end with Hart—it was only beginning. The Democratic candidate in 1992, Arkansas Governor Bill Clinton, brought with him a reputation for womanizing. Early in the campaign, the rumors of his affair with a younger woman, Gennifer Flowers, began to fly. Flowers herself claimed to have had an affair with Clinton lasting twelve years. Clinton ignored, then denied, the rumors. In the

PROMINENTLY DISPLAYED ALONGSIDE GENNIFER FLOWERS AT A **1992** PRESS CONFERENCE IN WHICH FLOWERS SPOKE OF HER ALLEGED AFFAIR WITH PRESIDENTIAL CANDIDATE BILL CLINTON IS THE FRONT PAGE OF THE *STAR*, A PRIME EXAMPLE OF TWENTIETH CENTURY "YELLOW" JOURNALISM.

meantime, he also dealt with accusations that he had dodged the draft during the Vietnam War.

Clinton survived the Gennifer Flowers problem and was elected in 1992. He was reelected in 1996. In the meantime, in the summer of 1995, his White House staff had accepted Monica Lewinsky as an intern. The real scandal was only beginning.

The Lewinsky Affair

Monica Lewinsky was the daughter of wealthy parents, a graduate of the private Bel Air Prep School in West Hollywood, and Lewis and Clark College in Portland, Oregon, majoring in psychology. Soon after arriving at the White House, she developed a crush on Bill Clinton, and her attention was returned. The president and Lewinsky began having sexual relations in the Oval Office. As the affair continued, Clinton grew concerned that the word would get out. He broke off the relationship and instructed his aides to see to it that Lewinsky got a well-paying federal job—away from the White House. In April 1997, Lewinsky moved on to a new job at the Pentagon.

Lewinsky confided her secret and her mixed emotions about the affair to another civilian Pentagon worker named Linda Tripp. Tripp secretly tape-recorded their telephone conversations. At Lewinsky's request, she kept evidence of the affair, including gifts the president had given Lewinsky.

MATT DRUDGE WAS THE FIRST TO BREAK THE STORY OF PRESIDENT CLINTON'S ALLEGED LIAISON WITH MONICA LEWINSKY IN HIS INTERNET NEWS DIARY, THE *DRUDGE REPORT*.

In early 1998, rumors of the Lewinsky affair were reaching the press. Members of the mainstream media, including Michael Isikoff of *Newsweek*, began investigating the story, tracking down sources and leads, and attempting to verify their information. The new Internet media, however, took a direct and faster approach—sources were unverified and rumors were given as much prominence as well-known facts.

Matt Drudge, in his Internet news digest known as the *Drudge Report*, was the first to break the news of the Lewinsky story and so, scooped the mainstream media. On January 17, 1998, the *Drudge Report* headlined its Web site with the following:

NEWSWEEK KILLS STORY ON WHITE HOUSE INTERN

BLOCKBUSTER REPORT: 23-YEAR OLD, FORMER WHITE HOUSE INTERN, SEX RELATIONSHIP WITH PRESIDENT

World Exclusive
Must Credit the DRUDGE REPORT

At the last minute, at 6 p.m. on Saturday evening, NEWSWEEK magazine killed a story that was destined to shake official Washington to its foundation: A White House intern carried on a sexual affair with the President of the United States!

The DRUDGE REPORT has learned that reporter Michael Isikoff developed the story of his career, only to have it spiked by top NEWSWEEK suits hours before publication . . .

Clinton had been dogged by rumors concerning his sex life ever since the 1992 campaign. An accusation of sexual harassment against him by a state employee named Paula Jones had even reached federal court. One of Jones's advisers, George Conway, tipped Drudge off to the *Newsweek* story, allowing Drudge to claim full credit for breaking the news to the public. Immediately after the Drudge story appeared, prosecutors in this case subpoenaed Lewinsky to testify. Lewinsky wrote and signed an affidavit swearing that she had never had sexual relations with the president. In the meantime, Clinton himself vigorously denied the rumors during testimony videotaped for the Jones trial.

The Lewinsky affair caused an instant media frenzy. *Newsweek*, *Time*, and every other major publication followed Drudge and covered the story, speculating on the truth or falsehood of the rumored affair. Clinton continued to deny the rumors until physical evidence that he was lying appeared in the form of a semen-stained blue dress, turned over to Linda Tripp by Monica Lewinsky. Eventually, charges of perjury and obstruction of justice led to Clinton's impeachment in the House of Representatives. He barely survived a vote to permanently remove him from office.

The story of Clinton and Lewinsky was matched by the story of the *Drudge Report* and *Newsweek* and the mainstream media. With the Lewinsky scandal, the Internet had found a groundbreaking national story, and a revolution in information was at hand. In the next few weeks, Drudge broke story after story connected to the affair, scooping the national media by simply reprinting rumors, tips, anonymous sources, unverified leads, and speculation. He also used printed and copyrighted stories by posting links to these stories on other media Web outlets. (Web users can freely click on links and read copyrighted stories, although some content must be purchased.)

Some of this information turned out to be true, some partially true, some simply false. This posed no problem for Drudge, who corrected inaccuracies when he felt like it and let the rest slide. The *Drudge Report* was accountable to no editor, no publisher, no parent company, and no advertisers. It ignored complaints from users and rivals. Its goal was simply public interest, as measured by the number of hits on its Web site.

Drudge developed enemies in the mainstream media. He was harshly criticized for using unverified sources and printing rumors and questionable information. He was attacked for playing to the public's prurient interest in the personal lives of public figures (who have to prove "actual malice" on the part of journalists in order to sue them for libel). Matt Drudge, pronounced some columnists, represented the worst aspects of journalism. He was irresponsible, unprofessional, and untruthful. The *Drudge Report*, in this view, was no better than the lowbrow yellow journalism that had flourished in the late nineteenth century.

Others took issue with the critics. They hailed Drudge for printing stories no one else dared, and for doing so faster than anyone else. They praised the *Drudge Report* as an admirable feat of Internet ingenuity, and as a vital expansion of available information media. They also pointed out Drudge's "democratization" of information. He had shown that anyone with a Web site and some imagination could provide the public with a vast amount of information. In the future, this meant that large private companies would no longer be the gatekeepers of news. The privileged few, in editors' offices and television studios, would lose their grip on the news. The public, as a result, would be better informed and would make better-informed decisions about their leaders.

In the end, the Lewinsky scandal paled beside Watergate. Clinton remained in office, and his approval ratings actually rose after his impeachment in Congress. His supporters denounced the affair as a media frenzy, and no more than the vindictive effort of political enemies to weaken

THIS PHOTO WAS USED BY KENNETH STARR IN HIS GOVERNMENT REPORT TO PROVE THAT PRESIDENT BILL CLINTON AND MONICA LEWINSKY HAD AN AFFAIR.

his administration—in the words of some, conservative revenge for Watergate. A flurry of opinion pieces decried the thirst for sex and scandal in the press, while Monica Lewinsky herself began hosting a cable-TV talk show.

The Personal Lives of Public Figures

Pro

• Public figures make themselves fair game for media investigation when they ask for the support of voters.
• The media have the right to uncover character flaws, as well as the right to investigate criminal activity. Such investigation allows the public to make an informed choice about the people for whom they are voting.
• The coverage of private lives places a check on personal misbehavior.

Con

• Public officials should be judged on their actions in office, not in their private lives, and reporters should keep out.
• Scandal is played up only for the sake of newsstand sales and broadcast ratings.
• Politicians use media scandals to make ad hominem (irrelevant) accusations and personal attacks on their rivals.
• Political campaigns turn into soap operas, and important public issues take a back seat.

6

Business and Government Control of Media

Many people will argue that a political bias exists in the media—a bias either to the "right" or "left"—depending on their own viewpoint. Others see a different problem: a bias toward uniformity and conformity. This bias does not allow those outside the mainstream to air their views. It does not allow news outlets to take risks, to criticize powerful institutions, or offend sponsors. This bias is more like cowardice than political prejudice. It has nothing to do with slanting information to one political side or the other. More than political bias, this media cowardice cheats the public out of useful and necessary information.

This bias originates in the control of media outlets by large and wealthy corporations, motivated solely by their own profit. In the late twentieth century, these corporations bought up media outlets, sometimes by the hundreds, bringing most television stations, radio stations, and newspapers under the control of just a few companies. Clear Channel, a radio broadcasting company, now controls more than 1,200 radio stations in the United States, and in some cities owns nearly every commercial station on the dial. Peter Phillips, in *Censored 2004*, comments:

> **Consolidation of media has brought the total news sources for most Americans to less than a handful, and these news groups have an ever-increasing dependency on prearranged content. The 24-hour news shows on MSNBC, Fox, and CNN are closely interconnected with various governmental and corporate sources for news.**

Like any other business, the company that owns television and radio stations, newspapers, magazines, or cable networks must make money to stay in business—preferably a steady and uninterrupted stream of money that grows with every passing year. The stream of money generated by media outlets comes from subscriptions and from advertising. The "product" on sale to the advertisers is an audience, which has many different sources of information to choose from. In theory, the audience reads or watches advertisements and is then persuaded to buy the product being advertised.

Advertisers pay large sums of money to have commercials run on television or print ads appear alongside newspaper or magazine articles. The advertisers want to reach the largest possible audience, which can be measured by circulation figures (for newspapers and magazines) and by television ratings. These ratings show the number of viewers and the share of the national audience captured by each program. Advertising takes up about 20 percent of the total time on commercial television stations and about

60 percent of all space in newspapers. Free media, such as radio and television broadcasts, earn all of their money from advertising.

As a result, advertising companies hold power over content. Their names and products are associated with the news and entertainment that accompany them. The influence of sponsors extends into content when products and logos (company symbols) appear on television shows, in sports broadcasts, or in movies. News anchors contribute to this even further by appearing in advertisements, pitching products to an audience that trusts them as people who gather and deliver the news.

Some advertisers want *all* business portrayed in a positive light. In a memo to television broadcasters, the multinational company Procter & Gamble, which spends billions a year on advertising, once decreed, "There will be no material that will give offense, either directly or indirectly to any commercial organization of any sort." Domino's Pizza went a little further with the variety show *Saturday Night Live*, pulling all of its advertising from the show because of what the company saw as an anti-Christian bias.

Advertising also plays a huge role in politics. "The media now defines who are serious political candidates," comments Phillips. "[W]hen [presidential candidate Ross Perot] promised to pour vast sums of his personal fortune into political advertising, he got major media coverage and the media got their payments for advertising. And then, of course, Perot got lots of free airtime."

Inoffensive Content

As a result, the advertisers want content that does not offend or upset the audience. They don't want programs that are critical of their own management or business practices, or the products they sell. They don't want to be associated with anything unpatriotic, illegal, distasteful, or immoral. If they don't like what they see, they can pull their ads and spend their dollars elsewhere.

Television producers and newspaper editors are well aware of this. As a result, they tailor their broadcasts and articles to keep them within acceptable limits for the sake of getting and keeping advertising money. Their employees carefully screen the scripts of TV shows as well as news stories. Anything considered offensive, or critical of an influential person or company, can be cut. Anything that might harm the network or newspaper itself, or help its competitors, can also be screened from public viewing. Television producers always consider the opinion of advertisers when creating a new show, or when reviewing a script.

While the Constitution bans censorship by the government, this "self-censorship," in the view of many, is just as harmful. It waters down entertainment content, making it bland, safe, and predictable, and keeping out controversial topics. It leaves news audiences less informed by not giving all sides of a debate, or by repressing news that might harm a sponsoring company. Advertisers want to reach an affluent audience, one with the ability to buy their products. To attract this audience and these advertisers, many programs give a distorted view of real life by emphasizing the lives and habits of the rich.

Advertisers have the right to be selective about media outlets they use. Ads are always tailored carefully to their potential audience. Sports broadcasts carry a lot of commercials for beer and cars—content geared towards men. Saturday morning cartoons feature the advertising of toys and games for children, while news broadcasts, watched by an older audience, tend to have prescription and over-the-counter drug companies as sponsors. Media executives also have the right to refuse advertising and be selective about what kind of ads they wish to run. But this selectivity can breed controversy. In May 2005, for the last episode of its reality show *Supernanny*, the ABC network sold advertising time to Focus on the Family, a conservative church group, while turning away ads for the United Church of Christ, a more liberal congregation.

Not everybody sees the influence of sponsors as necessarily a bad one. Advertising money from large corporations is what makes national media possible, as no individual or small company can afford the high costs of production and distribution. Advertising, in this view, is the oil that allows the media engine to run smoothly, to pay for new technologies, to produce high-quality shows, to operate foreign news bureaus, to disseminate information to a worldwide audience. Without advertising, the average consumer would have to pay much more for a newspaper, a magazine, or a cable subscription. And since watching television or reading a newspaper is voluntary, those who feel offended or uninformed by what they see or read can simply go somewhere else.

The only alternative would be to limit commercial sponsorship of television broadcasting, or to allow only public funding of the media through subscriptions or tax money. This would allow elected officials to control content and censor anything offensive or harmful to *them*. The result would be government control of information—the loss of a free press that is guaranteed by the Constitution.

Public Relations

Nearly all television and print news stories rely on information given out by businesses, organizations, and the government. Every big company and government agency has a department to handle this task. These media-relations or public-relations departments control the flow of information to the press. They grant permission for interviews, release statistics to the public, and describe their activities with "press releases."

The press release is a short statement, usually one or two pages long, that gives reporters information about the activities or decisions of an organization. Many press releases are simply bland statements, or a short version of a speech given by a representative or official. Some announce new products or services. Public officials give their positions on the issues with press releases. They describe laws in the making or explain important policy decisions.

Many reporters rely on press releases for background information. The activities of a company must be considered when reporting on that company. But some reporters depend on press releases for *all* their information. Out of laziness, or disinterest, or the desire not to offend an advertiser, they dig no further for information that might contradict an official version of events. They simply edit and reprint the press release as news. They may also take suggestions for stories directly from the company or an official, who may offer interviews and information to support the company's actions or point of view. The result is a story that is slanted in favor of a company that can create an effective press release.

A private company can take this process one step further by writing articles on its own and buying space in a newspaper to print the article. These "advertorials" appear as full-page ads or smaller, boxed ads on the opinion page of a newspaper. The ExxonMobil oil company frequently runs advertorials on the opinion pages of the *New York Times*. These pieces give ExxonMobil's opinion on the news. They describe the company's actions to protect the environment. They suggest policy—on energy, the environment, and other issues—to government officials. As long as ExxonMobil can pay for the space, the company has the right to express its views. Unfortunately, the advertorial appearing on a newspaper's editorial page can give the impression that it expresses the opinion of the newspaper itself. In effect, the newspaper simply becomes a mouthpiece for the company.

SUCCESSFUL PRESS SECRETARIES ARE USUALLY TALENTED AT MAKING OTHERS FEEL RELAXED. ARI FLEISHER, PRESS SECRETARY DURING THE FIRST TERM OF PRESIDENT GEORGE BUSH, JOKES WITH THE PRESS AFTER A SPEECH BY THE PRESIDENT WHILE HELPING OUT ONE OF THE CREW BY HOLDING THE TELEVISION CAMERA HIMSELF.

Government Control

By far the biggest public relations department in the United States belongs to the federal government. Every big government agency has a media relations office. The White House, the president, the members of the cabinet, and legislators all have press secretaries whose job is to convince the public, through the media, to support their employers. To win this support, the press office holds "background briefings" for reporters on important events. It releases "white papers," handily describing official policy on one matter or another. It arranges "photo opportunities," in which a high official is posed for photographers in a situation designed to make him or her look good.

The press secretary deals with reporters on a daily basis. Reporters look to the press office for information as well as access to officials for interviews. This access is vital—writing a story without interviewing people involved in the story is difficult, to say the least. To keep their access to powerful officials, reporters may avoid writing anything critical of them.

Government officials also control the news by leaking information. They call or meet with reporters and offer tips, rumors, or information "off the record." They ask not to be identified—a request that is usually honored by reporters who want to keep their sources. The information makes their opponents look bad, or is designed to help win public support of official policy.

To make their jobs easier, reporters may simply repeat what the government tells them, on or off the record. They may copy down press releases, transcribe official speeches, and try, in their own words, to explain what the government is doing and why. In this way, they become advocates for government policy. Because the federal government is such a powerful institution, it has the capability to get its side of the story heard—loud and clear.

In February 2004, the president of Haiti, Jean-Bertrand Aristide, fled his country when violent mobs swept through the streets of Port-au-Prince, the capital. The U.S. Department of State immediately claimed, in a press release, that Aristide had resigned and fled the country. Newspapers and television stations repeated the story. Soon afterward, however, Aristide called the Pacific News Service and claimed he had been kidnapped by U.S. and French Marines and forced onto a plane leaving Haiti.

Secretary of State Colin Powell emphatically denied that charge. Aristide then repeated his statements. At this point, finding the truth of the matter would be difficult. Reporters would have to interview Aristide, find witnesses to his actions in a violence-torn city, dig up evidence of U.S. intentions, and, if necessary, call the secretary of state a liar. Over the next few days, the story simply disappeared, with most newspapers presenting no evidence, one way or the other, of what really happened.

But television and newspapers aren't always kind to government. For the sake of a good story, the news media will seek out scandal, which draws the interest of the public, helps ratings and subscription numbers, and results in more advertising revenue. The Watergate scandal of 1974 ended with the resignation of President Richard Nixon. This was an important moment in media history, the first time that newspaper reporting had finished the career of a sitting president. Scandals also haunted President Ronald Reagan. In 1987, it was discovered that the Reagan White House was secretly selling arms to Iran, then an avowed enemy of the United States, and sending the money—illegally—to one side of a civil war in Nicaragua. President Bill Clinton also got unwanted attention in the 1990s, when newspapers and television stations played up his relationship with Lewinsky. In 2005, a war scandal broke out as the

SUPPORTERS OF FORMER PRESIDENT JEAN-BERTRAND ARISTIDE DEMAND HIS RETURN DURING A MARCH 2004 DEMONSTRATION NEAR THE PRESIDENTIAL PALACE IN PORT-AU-PRINCE.

media investigated the conduct of the second attack on Iraq in 2003, finding that much of the evidence laid out by the administration of President George W. Bush was false or distorted.

Many complain about the taste for government scandal among news reporters. Those whose side—Republican or Democrat—is affected by scandal see media misbehavior. In their opinion, the media too often rely on sensation and distortion to attract and amuse the public. Those whose political enemies are under attack see the situation differently. They feel upset that the media don't do more investigation, and complain when the story fades from the front page.

The Hostile Media

In the debate over media, liberal and conservative partisans agree on one thing: the media stand against them. For conservatives, the media have an overwhelming liberal bias. The majority of reporters are liberal, and so are most newspapers, magazines, and television stations. The news is slanted against conservatives, who are always described as "right-wing" or "conservative" in the news (while the label "liberal" is avoided—to make liberals appear more normal and mainstream). The right wing is associated with intolerant bigots, greedy capitalists, and the "religious right." Conservatives believe that left-wing media bias is an important reason for the creation of new information sources, such as the Fox News Channel and the Drudge Report.

To liberals, the media are, without a doubt, conservative. Big corporations control the vast majority of newspapers and broadcast media, and these corporations are owned and operated by the wealthy—who are mostly conservatives. Reporters may be liberal, but their editors and publishers are conservative and they control content. Major social and environmental problems are glossed over. Military actions by the United States are supported without question. Centrist viewpoints are represented as "liberal" by the media, who rarely offer true liberals a forum to speak their minds. The media paint liberals as extreme and out-of-touch with common people. Their opinions are ridiculed as being "politically incorrect" and intolerant. Liberal politicians are dogged by media scandal and innuendo, while conservatives are portrayed as tough-minded, capable, patriotic, and family-oriented.

This "hostile media effect" allows each side to claim unfairness. It allows people to point to any news unfavorable to their side and blame the media for distortion. Because the media are so powerful, it also allows both sides

Fairness and the Rules

Many laws and rules have been written to ensure fairness in the media. These regulations date to 1934, when Congress passed the Communications Act. Section 315 of this law stated that radio stations must offer "equal opportunity" to all political candidates. Policy changed again in 1939, when the conservative Yankee Network ran on-air editorials against President Franklin Roosevelt, a Democrat. When the competing Mayflower Network applied to the Federal Communications Commission (FCC) to take over one of Yankee's New York radio stations, Mayflower claimed that the Yankee broadcasters were not allowing a fair balance of views on the air. The FCC allowed the Yankee network to keep its station on the condition that it stop editorializing. With this Mayflower Doctrine, the FCC banned stations from making editorial comments of their own on public issues or candidates.

This rule proved impossible to enforce, however, as it was a violation of the right to free speech. The FCC began asking radio stations instead to air balanced views of public issues, a policy that became known as the Fairness Doctrine. As a "public trust," broadcasters held their FCC licenses for the benefit of the public. As a result, they are required to inform the public of important issues, and try to air competing opinions whenever possible. The rule was rarely enforced, but broadcasters often complained about it. They believed the presentation of viewpoints should be up to them, and that no government agency had the right to tell them what to broadcast. According to this view, this law also violated their free-speech rights under the First Amendment.

The Fairness Doctrine was abandoned during the 1980s, an important era for information media. Congress and the FCC deregulated the media business—old laws and rules were dropped. Because many new media outlets were appearing, especially cable TV stations, differing viewpoints became easier to find. It didn't seem so important to ensure that every television or radio station present a balanced view. In 1987, the FCC officially dropped the Fairness Doctrine.

Bias in the media is still a cause for loud public complaint. According to the Museum of Broadcasting Web site, "the fairness doctrine remains just beneath the surface of concerns over broadcasting and cablecasting, and some members of Congress continue to threaten to pass it into legislation. Currently, however, there is no required balance of controversial issues as mandated by the fairness doctrine. The public relies instead on the judgment of broadcast journalists and its own reasoning ability to sort out one-sided or distorted coverage of an issue."

to claim underdog status—and win sympathy from ordinary people. The "hostile media effect" is easy and very convenient for both sides. It is the subject of hundreds of books and magazine articles and of constant debate.

The truth of media "bias" comes down to the perception of each individual toward what he or she hears or reads. In the United States, broadcast networks and newspapers are free to give information, or slant information, any way they want. Readers and viewers have a choice, and everyone has access to information, from thousands of sources. Individuals can make up their own minds and accept or reject what they hear, see, or read. A well-informed individual can plainly see true bias. Those who subscribe to the "hostile media effect," whether liberal or conservative, give the average person little credit for such perception and intelligence.

The Media and War

Reporting during wartime stirs up emotions. When the country fights battles overseas, the public pays close attention to news reports. The press covers the war with large staffs of journalists and photographers assigned exclusively to the story. Network television hires expert commentators to talk about military tactics, weaponry, and the chances of defeat or victory.

In media coverage of any war, bias comes into play. Newspapers may root for the government—encouraging the nation to go to war, celebrating victories, and lamenting defeats. This was the case in World War II, which the United States entered in 1941 against Germany and Japan. The public largely supported the war, and most press accounts described it as a fight against the evil tyranny of Nazi Germany and Imperial Japan. Important battles won by the United States were celebrated in newspapers, and the final victory in 1945 inspired banner headlines.

But the media can also be critical of war. Editors may run stories highlighting the incompetence of, and poor decisions made by, the military. The Vietnam War, for example, was controversial from the start. In the early 1960s, the United States sent military advisers and then ground troops to South Vietnam to help the South Vietnamese government fight a Communist insurgency. The war rapidly escalated, with the United States building huge military bases and bombing targets in South and North Vietnam, Cambodia, and Laos from the air. Some saw the United States valiantly fighting a Communist threat to Southeast Asia—others saw the U.S. government making war on a poor Asian country and foolishly interfering in a civil war.

The Vietnam War began a new era of media war coverage. For the first time, television cameras were present on the field of battle. Every evening, images of the war were beamed into living rooms on the network news. Those opposed to the war had their opinion bolstered by televised battles full of blood, chaos, and death. These violent images, body counts on the nightly news, and the televised arrival of coffins carrying American soldiers brought the reality of the war a little closer to home.

The war brought close attention and heavy criticism to press coverage. Those who supported the war believed that negative press reports were hurting an important effort in a good cause. They believed the media were purposely manipulating the public against the war. The accounts of civilian casualties, and of massacres committed by American soldiers, made the war look more like a crime than a noble effort to turn back Communism.

The War and Cable

Eventually, a loss of public support convinced the American government to withdraw from Vietnam. Soon afterward, South Vietnam fell to a Communist government, a defeat that stung the military and made the U.S. government reluctant to commit troops to battle abroad. For the next fifteen years, the U.S. military stayed home, except for brief campaigns in Grenada, Panama, and Lebanon.

Then came the Gulf War conflict between the United States and Iraq in 1991. After Iraq's President Saddam Hussein ordered an invasion of Kuwait in August 1990, U.S. President George H. W. Bush vowed to liberate the country from the Iraqi army. In January 1991, the war began with a monthlong bombardment, holding the rapt attention of the nation. CNN responded with around-the-clock war coverage. The network broadcast daily battlefield reports while military experts gave opinions from television studios, using colorful maps and graphics to provide a video-enhanced play-by-play of the war. CNN's audience ratings increased dramatically.

CNN's coverage of the Gulf War brought accusations of bias from supporters and opponents of the war. Those critical of the war accused the network of cooperating closely with the U.S. government in order to gain access to military officials, and permission for its reporters to follow the story from the fronts. The war, in this view, was being presented under the control of the U.S. administration and military. Instead of a free and open press, coverage was provided by an obedient handmaiden of the military.

Others saw the situation quite differently. They believed CNN reporters personally opposed the war and allowed their bias to influence their reporting. One CNN reporter, Peter Arnett, drew much of the criticism. Arnett's reporting, in the eyes of some, was downright hostile to the United States and its efforts against Saddam Hussein.

In the opening hours of the war, Arnett, along with Bernard Shaw and John Holliman, reported from a hotel room in the Iraqi capital of Baghdad. In dramatic fashion, Arnett recounted the sights and sounds of the initial bombardment of the city by American warplanes. The reporting gave viewers a vicarious thrill, the feeling of being present at a historic, and very dangerous, event.

The situation, in the eyes of CNN producers, soon became too dangerous for their reporters. The network pulled Holliman and Shaw out of Iraq, leaving Arnett the sole American reporter remaining inside the country. For five weeks, Arnett held center stage at the first war in history broadcast live on television. He interviewed civilians, military officers, and Saddam Hussein himself. But his reporting did not always cast a very pleasant view on the war's effects. Arnett's reports of damages among civilians seemed to contradict the military's claim that "smart bombs" were largely sparing civilian lives. When a factory on the outskirts of Baghdad was destroyed by American bombs, Arnett arrived on the scene to claim that the United States had just demolished a facility for manufacturing infant formula. The administration disagreed, claiming that Iraq was using the factory to make biological weapons.

On January 25, the White House accused Arnett and CNN of acting as tools of Iraqi propaganda. Thirty-four members of Congress signed a letter of protest, accusing Arnett of unpatriotic reporting. The controversy did little to harm CNN. Arnett himself became one of the stars of the war, a center of controversy and a lightning rod for those who accused the media and in particular, CNN, of liberal bias.

The Second Iraq War

The Iraq war, like Vietnam, divided public opinion. Some supported the war as a noble effort aimed at rooting out terrorism in the Middle East. Others saw it as an effort by the United States to occupy and control Iraq. The government of the United States claimed to be fighting a war on terrorism, and to be seeking democratic change in a part of the world suffering from many years of tyranny.

Around the world, the war stirred debate and opposition. Media reports of events in Iraq inspired angry reactions. In many Muslim countries, the occupation of a Muslim land by the army of a (largely) Christian nation was met with anger, riots, and terrorism. Small and violent incidents turned into international events, covered closely by the press around the world. Stories were seized on by both sides as justification for their opinions.

In the United States, press coverage of the war became an issue between liberals, who generally opposed the war, and conservatives, who generally supported it. War supporters believed the press was playing up military setbacks. They criticized coverage of conditions at American military prisons. In 2004, photographs of U.S. soldiers torturing and humiliating Muslim prisoners at Abu Ghraib prison, twenty miles west of the Iraqi capital of Baghdad, caused a worldwide scandal. Press reports of the U.S. prison at Guantanamo, in Cuba, also brought criticism of the war.

In late 2004, the Guantanamo prison caught the interest of a *Newsweek* reporter, Michael Isikoff, who had

AN AL-QAEDA DETAINEE (IN ORANGE) IS ESCORTED BY U.S. MILITARY PERSONNEL AT THE GUANTANAMO BAY NAVAL BASE ON JANUARY 17, 2002.

investigated the Monica Lewinsky story in 1998. He had heard reports of abuse at the prison and knew that the military was investigating these reports. Isikoff contacted an anonymous source in the government. The source told him that the government report would include new details. Isikoff included some of these details in a draft of a short story about Guantanamo. His story was then given to an official at the Department of Defense. The official reviewed the story, and did not deny the details.

Setting off a Riot

On May 9, *Newsweek* ran a short item in Periscope, a section of short articles on current events and politics. "SouthCom Showdown" described the interrogation of Muslim prisoners at Guantanamo, an American military base on the island of Cuba. According to the stories, American interrogators were humiliating these prisoners in several different ways: "Among the previously unreported cases, sources tell *Newsweek*: interrogators, in an attempt to rattle suspects, flushed a Koran [the Muslim holy book] down a toilet and led a detainee around with a collar and dog leash."

There were no further details. There were no further interviews, no witnesses, and no confirmation of the stories by a second party. There had already been many media stories about abuse of Iraqi and Muslim prisoners by the United States. The desecration of the Koran had featured in several of them. But this time, the story "caught fire." It was picked up and repeated, in newspapers and television broadcasts, and on the Internet, all over the world—particularly the Muslim world. The article became, in itself, the story.

In Pakistan and Afghanistan, the unconfirmed, unwitnessed details created a furor. Political leaders allied with the United States found themselves under attack. On May 6, a

INDIAN MUSLIMS HOLD UP THE KORAN DURING AN ANTI-U.S. DEMON-
STRATION IN BOMBAY ON MAY 16, 2005. THE DEMONSTRATORS
WERE ANGRY AT *NEWSWEEK*'S RETRACTION OF THE STORY, BELIEVING
THAT GOVERNMENT PRESSURE FORCED THE MAGAZINE TO SAY THAT ITS
ALLEGATIONS OF DESECRATION OF THE KORAN BY THE U.S. MILITARY
WERE FALSE.

well-known Pakistani athlete, Imran Khan, held up a copy of *Newsweek* and denounced the United States for the abuse of the Koran at Guantanamo. Religious leaders throughout Pakistan followed Khan's lead—and harshly criticized their own president, Pervez Musharraf, for helping the United States in the "war on terrorism."

In Afghanistan, opponents of President Hamid Karzai, who allied himself closely with the United States, seized on the *Newsweek* story to discredit him. The desecration of the Koran was considered a grave insult and humiliation to all Muslims everywhere. Riots broke out, the worst in Kabul, the capital of Afghanistan. Angry mobs in Kabul burned American flags, overturned cars,

AFGHANS GATHER NEAR A VEHICLE BURNT BY PROTESTERS IN JALALABAD ON MAY 11, 2005.

broke windows, and confronted the police. More than a dozen people were killed.

The Pentagon then contacted *Newsweek* to say the story was inaccurate. *Newsweek* ran a retraction—a short article admitting that its story was probably false. The retraction did not satisfy many people, who saw the *Newsweek* article as one more example of unfair media bias against the war. *Newsweek* then covered reaction to its own story two weeks later in a three-page article entitled "How a Fire Broke Out":

> **By the end of the week, the rioting had spread from Afghanistan throughout much of the Muslim world, from Gaza to Indonesia. Mobs shouting 'Protect our Holy Book!' burned down government buildings and ransacked the offices of relief organizations in several Afghan provinces.**

At home, *Newsweek* got most criticism from conservatives, who believed the magazine was intentionally undermining the war effort. A critic of *Newsweek*, L. Brent Bozell, believed that the magazine was directly responsible for the deaths in Afghanistan. Writing on the Media Research Center Web site, Bozell commented that:

> **[T]he story, left unchallenged, would prove highly damaging to the Bush administration . . . If U.S. military interrogators were really stupid enough to think it's a neat idea to get information from Islamic radicals by flushing their sacred texts in the rest room, the White House would be confirmed as reckless zealots declaring war on every Islam-dominated nation. At this writing, the death toll caused by the *Newsweek* story stands at 17.**

The War on Terrorism garnered some negative coverage from entertainers on television. After the terrorist attacks of 2001, Bill Maher, on his television show *Politically Incorrect*, stated, "we have been the cowards lobbing cruise missiles from 2,000 miles away. That's cowardly. Staying in the airplane when it hits the building, say what you want about it, it's not cowardly." Maher came in for his share of criticism from the press and the public for his remarks. Two major sponsors pulled their advertising from the show, and seventeen local cable outlets stopped running it. *Politically Incorrect* survived the controversy for a few months before it was cancelled in 2002.

Things were much the same in the spring of 1969, when the administration of Richard Nixon came in for some heavy satire on *The Smothers Brothers Comedy Hour*, a popular CBS prime-time television show. Dick and Tommy Smothers played to a younger audience by making fun of the Vietnam War, the military, the Nixon administration, and organized religion. But they also brought complaints from viewers upset that a show advertised as a "variety show," that is, meant for entertainment only—would have *any* political content.

Unhappy with the complaints, the network demanded that the show be submitted for review before it aired. The network censors deleted lines and entire skits. CBS executives fought a continual battle with the Smothers Brothers over their "anti-establishment" attitude and irreverent comedy. Finally, in late March, the network cancelled the show entirely, claiming that the Smothers Brothers had failed to deliver their tapes in time for review. In fact, network executives were fed up with the show's constant controversies.

The decision was supported by the country's most popular television magazine, *TV Guide*. In an editorial after the cancellation, *TV Guide* opined: "Where does satire end—and sacrilege begin? Where does criticism end—and affront begin? Where does disagreement end—and national division begin? . . . The issue is: Shall entertainers using a mass medium for all the people be allowed to amuse a few by satirizing religion while offending the substantial majority?"

Commentator Kenneth A. Paulson wrote:

> **The right to offend may be guaranteed by the First Amendment right to free speech. But as Maher and the Smothers Brothers discovered, starting a political controversy in a medium designed for entertainment can have unhappy results.**

High-Level Reaction

The White House had its share of criticism for *Newsweek* as well. A White House spokesman, Scott McClellan, publicly slammed the magazine, saying the retraction was only a "first step" to undoing the damage the article had done. McClellan asked that *Newsweek* go further, by writing a story explaining how, exactly, the false story had been allowed to pass into print. McClellan also asked that the magazine explain the policy of the U.S. military and its guidelines on treating prisoners and their religion.

The White House spokesman was supported by allied members of Congress. One representative urged every member of Congress to cancel his or her subscription to *Newsweek*. Another, Representative Deborah Pryce of Ohio, stated that "retraction and regrets will not atone for the reckless behavior of an irresponsible reporter and an overzealous publication."

Newsweek editors fired back, and a war of words ensued. The editors said they had double-checked their sources, admitted their mistake, and printed a retraction—standard procedure when a newspaper or magazine gets its facts wrong. The editors also indignantly refused to take orders from the White House. They would not print stories that only benefited or praised the U.S. government, the military, the war, or the president.

The *Newsweek* article set off an avalanche of commentary in print and broadcast media. Conservatives seized on it as one more example, among many, of deep-seated liberal bias in the dominant media. Liberals reacted by accusing conservatives of ignoring the Bush administration's own deceptions, particularly in the stated reasons for the war, the goals of the war, and the success of the war.

One liberal commentator, Tom Teepen, remarked: "Conservatives endlessly bellyache about the supposed liberal bias of every newspaper, magazine, or TV network that is not overtly on their side. Liberal has been redefined as any utterance that is not markedly conservative."

The close attention any war brings heightens the debate over media bias. Any event in wartime can be distorted by what is described, and what is ignored, and by the terms used to describe the event. While some see a war of liberation, others see occupation. When some see legitimate treatment of dangerous prisoners, others see abuse and scandal. As the war continues, opponents can see a Vietnamlike "morass," and lives lost in a hopeless cause. Supporters see a noble effort and insist on support of the war and the military as a patriotic act. Both sides, at all times, see an unfair slant to the news they read and watch.

War Coverage

Pro

- Television coverage of war brings its death and fear directly into the living room, allowing people to see its grim reality.
- During wartime, the media is spurred on to deeper investigation of the workings of government and the military, and becomes a forum for more meaningful debate on the nation's ideals and ethos.
- By using a variety of media sources, the public can better gauge the success or failure of military operations, and disregard the slanted information and propaganda supplied by the government.

Con

- Television trivializes war and turns it into cheap living-room entertainment.
- Television is used by authority figures to more effectively sell their reasons for going to war.
- Inaccuracies in media reports—such as false reporting of casualties or atrocities—cause trouble by swaying the public against military missions. Also, news reports can reveal troop movements and strategy, compromising the efforts of the military.

Public Broadcasting

Public broadcasting, supported by tax dollars, subscriptions, and contributions, is common outside of the United States. In the United Kingdom, the public British Broadcasting Corporation (BBC) is the dominant television and radio network, with several different channels catering to a variety of interests. In many other nations, governments control the airwaves entirely and don't allow private use of radio or television transmissions. Some of these public stations serve as propaganda arms for their governments. Censors control the programming, allowing no criticism or ridicule of the government.

In the United States, public broadcasting began with the Voice of America, a radio network owned and operated by the government. Founded in 1942, during World War II, the VOA broadcast to countries occupied by Nazi Germany in Europe and North Africa. After the war's end in

THOUGH THE WINDS IN BROADCASTING ARE INCREASINGLY CONSERVATIVE, ONE NEW LIBERAL OUTPOST HAS CROPPED UP ON THE AIR: AIR AMERICA, A LIBERAL TALK RADIO STATION, DEBUTED IN 2004 TO COMBAT WHAT SOME LIBERALS SEE AS THE NEW CONSERVATIVE BROADCAST BIAS.

1945, the VOA continued broadcasting around the world, providing information and news reports that generally supported the actions and goals of the United States. The VOA targeted the Soviet Union and Communist central Europe beginning in 1947. By a federal law passed in 1948, the VOA cannot broadcast directly to U.S. citizens. The law was meant to prevent the government from using the network as a propaganda forum in the United States.

The success of the VOA partially inspired the founding of the Corporation for Public Broadcasting (CPB) in 1967 during the presidency of Lyndon Johnson. The CPB in turn founded the Public Broadcasting System (PBS) in 1969. With seed money from the CPB, PBS television stations, as well as National Public Radio (NPR) stations, were established in major cities all over the country. PBS produced shows meant to be educational and informative, and free of commercial advertising. By far the most popular was *Sesame Street*, a children's educational show.

President Johnson may have signed the bill giving birth to CPB, but he didn't always appreciate what the bill produced. Criticism of the Vietnam War, which Johnson oversaw and supported, appeared regularly on PBS programs. One reporter in particular, Bill Moyers, often irritated Johnson over Vietnam. Moyers had been a press secretary for Johnson, but after leaving the administration in 1967 began to sharply criticize the war. After Richard Nixon won the presidency in the 1968 elections, Moyers kept up his attack. His PBS reports on Watergate and other issues that embarrassed Nixon made him a favorite target of the president, who pressured CPB to get Moyers off the air.

PBS stations have been supported by money from the CPB—which has an annual budget of $400 million—as well as fund drives. But every year, Congress must renew government funding of CPB. As lawmakers debate the federal budget, some raise the issue of public broadcasting. Some are displeased by what they see as bias on PBS and NPR programs. Some don't want tax money paying for television and radio broadcasting at all. During the 1990s, Republican senators proposed abolishing the CPB. They were met with an outcry from supporters of public broadcasting, and CPB survived. But the debate surrounding public broadcasting stayed alive into the twenty-first century.

Why Public Media?

Many believe that public broadcasting serves an essential purpose. As they are free of commercials, PBS shows don't have to bow to the demands of advertisers, who only use the media to sell their products and who want television that is free of troubling questions, true debate, and controversy. In addition, public stations are independent of private media corporations, with their many affiliated companies, that might hand down programming directives or exert pressure to portray them in the best possible light. Public stations can also give air time to a wider range of views, and provide a forum for lengthy, in-depth analysis and debate.

A contrary view holds that government should not be funding public entertainment or information media. This view sees a more proper use of tax money in paying for more essential government functions. Many opponents of public broadcasting also believe that it tends to have a liberal political bias. They point out the anti-conservative bias in programs such as *Frontline*, a weekly PBS documentary, *NewsHour with Jim Lehrer*, and *NOW*. They also see liberal bias in *All Things Considered*, a news production carried on stations affiliated with National Public Radio.

Many of those who see conservative bias in commercial television criticize big corporations owning TV and radio networks and print media. They have another problem also: corporate sponsorship of public broadcasting. In the 1970s, many large companies began donating money to support individual programs. The Mobil Oil Company, for example, sponsored *Masterpiece Theater*, a British production that was popular with critics and audiences.

Every week, the Mobil advertising logo appeared with a short announcement before the program. Large oil companies followed Mobil's example, supporting nearly three-fourths of public television by 1981. "The sad truth," write media critics Martin Lee and Norman Solomon in their book *Unreliable Sources*, "is that PBS and National Public Radio (NPR) are 'made possible' to large degree by the same corporate sponsors that bring us commercial programming."

Like commercial advertisers, Mobil and other underwriters (sponsors) of public TV shows seek a large audience, wealthy enough to become steady and reliable customers. They want the shows they sponsor to attract this audience, and show producers, in turn, want to attract more money from underwriters. The possible result is programming geared to a particular social and ethnic group. In this way, some critics point out, corporate underwriters have become the advertisers in public broadcasting, and they have the same influence as advertisers in commercial media—they tend to water down the programming and make it more "mainstream."

A New Chairman of the Board

Conservatives have often pushed elected officials to end tax funding for the Corporation for Public Broadcasting. They believed that PBS and public broadcasting should be able to survive on contributions from viewers and members—who, if they wanted such broadcasting, should be willing to support it. Taxpayers who didn't support public broadcasting, or who saw in it a bias they didn't like, should not be forced to help pay for it.

Conservatives had another answer in the form of new, conservative PBS programming: *The Journal Editorial Report*, a news show with all-conservative panelists, and *Tucker Carlson Unfiltered*, a show hosted by a conservative commentator who had worked for several years on CNN.

These shows were ushered into the PBS lineup by Kenneth Y. Tomlinson. A conservative Republican, Tomlinson saw what was then *Now with Bill Moyers* as unfairly dominating the Friday evening lineup of PBS shows. He believed that *NOW* (as it is currently called) was the prime

TUCKER CARLSON IS A CONSERVATIVE COMMENTATOR WHO HAS COME TO PROMINENCE IN THE LAST SEVERAL YEARS.

example of liberal bias on public television, and that such a show was damaging PBS's standing among the public. To bolster his argument, in 2004 Tomlinson hired an outside consultant to watch the show and carefully measure the extent of liberal bias displayed by Moyers in his news reports and commentaries, and in the guests he chose to appear on the show.

Tomlinson had once served on the editorial board of *Reader's Digest* and as the chairman of the Voice of America. He became chairman of the board of the Corporation for Public Broadcasting in September 2003. Tomlinson supported conservative programming on PBS, claiming only that he sought a balanced mix of views on the network. This idea drew the approval of many conservative critics of PBS, including President George Bush.

Tomlinson pushed for new, conservative-leaning shows to counteract what he saw as liberal bias. He hired a former head of the Republican National Committee, Patricia Harrison, as president of PBS, and the head of the White House Office of Global Communications, Mary Catherine Andrews, to set up a new office of ombudsman. The job of the two ombudsmen would be to review the content of television and radio broadcasts, hear public complaints, and address the issue of bias. In addition, new ground rules were put in place for CPB productions and programming.

The new, conservative emphasis at the Corporation for Public Broadcasting drew heavy fire from critics on the left. They see PBS and NPR becoming a propaganda arm of the conservative Republican Party and the Bush administration, rather than a public service. Tomlinson's guidelines and ombudsmen, in this view, would kill public broadcasting journalism. News reporters would avoid questioning or investigating government actions, and news producers would allow criticism of Republican officials only at the risk of their jobs.

One harsh critic of Tomlinson, Jonathan Chait, came around to the old conservative proposal: end government funding of CPB entirely. In the *Los Angeles Times*, Chait explained that "the only real way to kill public broadcasting is to subject it to political manipulation. And the only way to guarantee that doesn't happen is to free public broadcasting from the government."

Tomlinson's actions also caused a furor among PBS affiliates, the local public television stations that pick up much of their programming from CPB-sponsored productions. It also caused a major problem with television producers, including David Fanning, the executive producer of *Frontline*. Fanning commented that Tomlinson's actions were "designed to get people's attention and warn them not to do programming that will be questioned . . . We ask hard questions to people in power. That's anathema to some people in Washington these days."

Tomlinson defended his actions as being in the best interest of PBS and of public broadcasting. He stated that public trust in PBS as an unbiased source of information was essential to its survival. "My goal here is to see programming that satisfies a broad constituency. I'm not after removing shows or tampering internally with shows."

The Future of Public Broadcasting

As media evolved and audiences had more information sources in the form of cable news networks and the Internet, the role of public broadcasting came into question. In the past, when only three private, commercial television networks were available, public broadcasting represented an important alternative.

At the start of the twenty-first century, a very different media world existed. Commercial stations still relied on advertising for support, but there were hundreds of these stations available to anyone with a cable-TV subscription. Some were entertainment channels, some were sports channels, and some were news channels. There were food channels, childrens' channels, a history channel, movie channels, and channels that played decades-old television programs.

The abundance of specialized channels brings the usefulness of public broadcasting into question. For many critics of public TV and radio, there is less need for a network offering commercial-free programming—no matter what its political bias or lack of bias. And government funding of such programming inevitably brings a pro-government bias, as the political party in power appoints its friends to run the Corporation for Public Broadcasting. The use of tax money to support such broadcasting seems questionable.

For these critics, public support of broadcasting networks should come in the form of voluntary contributions. PBS should be supported by subscriptions and fund drives, and it should give up the use of tax money. If it can survive in this way, and remain commercial-free, well and good. If it can't survive on voluntary donations, it should close up shop.

Supporters of publicly financed broadcasting see things in a very different light. They want continuing tax support as a way of lessening the influence of big corporate donors. Since these companies can donate much more than an individual, they have a bigger say in what gets put on the air. They discourage programming that might cast them in a negative light, while individual viewers have no influence over programming at all. Public television becomes an imitation of commercial television, while the original point was to provide an alternative to it.

Public Television, Public Support?

Pro

- Public television allows in-depth news and innovative entertainment programming not seen on commercial television.
- Commercial-free television and radio programs provide more enjoyable viewing and listening. Children's programming on public stations also spares kids from the endless food and toy advertisements on commercial networks.
- The influence of advertising sponsors on programming decisions is less.
- Public television can provide a forum for a wider range of views.

Con

- Tax money should not be used to support public broadcasting, as many taxpayers don't use it or approve of it.
- The government is not in the entertainment business. That is the role of private media companies who must survive without public money.
- Inevitably, public officials will try to use public media to propagandize for themselves and their political leanings.
- Public television should be able to survive on its own in a new media world, in which the Internet and cable television provide a much wider range of choices.

9
A Biased Future

No longer restricted to three major networks, the information media have splintered into thousands of new outlets in broadcast and cable television, print sources, and the Internet. The concept of "open source" media means that control of information is moving out of the hands of large organizations and into the hands of individuals. In the twenty-first century, new information sources will be constantly created, packaged, and sold to consumers, a process that speeds up as new technologies appear on the market.

Media consumers no longer depend on publication and broadcast schedules. They can record and play back television programming to fit their interests and their schedule. They can access favorite Web sites at any time, and create their own Weblogs to provide commentary on the news. In the near future, an individual will be able to

THE FUTURE OF THE MEDIA, LIBERAL AND CONSERVATIVE, MAY LIE WITH THE INTERNET. PICTURED IS THE WEB SITE OF RADIQRADIO.COM, WHICH WAS CREATED TO CHALLENGE THE MALAYSIAN GOVERNMENT'S TIGHT GRIP ON PRINT AND BROADCAST MEDIA.

tailor his or her own cable TV lineup, limiting it to stations focusing on more personal interests. The viewer will order news and entertainment "on demand," at the most convenient time, and bring it to a wider range of content receivers: handheld sets, mobile phones, and private screens that can be operated anywhere. Of course, those who buy TIVO can do that at least now, to some extent. Individuals will also be able to *create* programming by collecting video, music, and text on a personal Web page and then offering it for consumption around the globe.

One of the major complaints about media is its control by large and wealthy corporations. In the past, television programming required large investments of money and sophisticated equipment—in addition to a broadcasting license from the Federal Communications Commission. As the platform for television production moves to the Internet, the cost of programming will fall. Smaller companies and individuals will be able to compete with CNN and the broadcast networks for viewers. As the audience shrinks for these "mainstream media" outlets, they will feel the pressure to create programming for a segmented, rather than mass, audience.

Even as the media expands and fragments, the hold of two major political parties over elections and government will remain. These two parties, Democrat and Republican, conveniently represent liberal and conservative sides to most voters and political analysts. In the future, the parties may have their own media outlets to offer their take on events and issues. Politicians will no longer have to contend with the "filter" of major media outlets, and their reporters, to get their message across. The Democrat channel and the Republican channel will be available around the clock, presenting candidates and opinions with their unmistakable political bias. This has been the case for generations in Europe, where all major newspapers have a known political identity.

New technologies will change the debate over bias in the media. Many already see this debate as a relic of media history. When content was under the control of a few media companies, viewers and readers had good reason for complaint, as they had no control over how and when information was broadcast. The media's claim to objective reporting came under constant attack, and every important issue saw a fierce argument over perceived bias in coverage and commentary.

As it splinters programming further, new television will cater to narrower interests on the part of viewers. Claims of balance and objectivity will grow faint; instead, media outlets will trumpet their biases in order to attract a larger share of a splintered audience. The debate over bias, and complaints of media concentration, will remain loudest for the most powerful newspapers, those with a national audience: the *New York Times*, the *Wall Street Journal*, *USA Today*, and the *Washington Post*. Because the production and distribution of these sources remain in the hands of large companies, catering to a mass audience, they will become the last bastion of traditional, twentieth century journalism, which aspired to present "just the facts," free of bias. But their claims will fall on deaf ears: because they are so powerful, people take the stories and opinions published in these newspapers more seriously, and object much louder if their point of view is challenged.

As a result, the "hostile media effect" will survive, as partisans of the right and left point out that the media are slanted against their side. But the options for contending with it will increase. Weblogs and Internet information services will bypass commercial television and radio as well as national newspapers such as the *New York Times* and the *Wall Street Journal*. Since most Internet sites survive with minimal advertising, they feel no pressure to moderate their views to attract a wider audience, raise money, and compete with other sites. Instead, they compete with the presentation of extreme views, outlandish claims, biased reporting, rumor, innuendo, and outright slander—the more outrageous, the better—to intrigue Internet surfers searching for something notable among the thousands of available news sites.

A more important question will be society's ability to compromise and agree on pressing issues—social and economic policy, taxes, trade, the environment, immigration, foreign affairs, military action. With hundreds of admittedly biased media outlets contending for attention, the views of someone who disagrees can be more easily ignored. The inability to understand an opponent's views, and to find some common ground for action, brings public apathy and political paralysis—serious drawbacks in dealing with any problem.

Notes

Chapter 1

p. 11, Darrell West, *The Rise and Fall of the Media Establishment*. New York: Palgrave Macmillan, 2001, p. 11.

p. 13, Fawn Brodie. *Thomas Jefferson: An Intimate History*. New York: W. W. Norton, 1974, p. 349.

p. 13, Brodie, p. 10.

p. 14, Neil Gabler. *Life: The Movie: How Entertainment Conquered Reality*. New York: Vintage Books, 2000, p. 60.

p. 16, Gabler, p. 29.

p. 16, E. L. Godkin, "Journalistic Dementia," *Nation*, March 14, 1895, pp. 195–196.

Chapter 2

p. 23, Neil Postman, *Amusing Ourselves to Death: Public Discourse in the Age of Show Business*. New York: Penguin Books, 1986, pp. 8 and 51.

p. 28, "A Star from Mosul," http://astarfrommosul.blogspot.com/2004_06_01_astarfrommosul_archive.html (Accessed July 1, 2005.)

p. 29, "Lott Apologizes for Thurmond Comment," CNN.com, December 10, 2002, http://archives.cnn.com/2002/ALLPOLI-TICS/12/09/lott.comment. (Accessed December 8, 2005.)

p. 33, Corey Pein, "Blog-Gate," *Columbia Journalism Review* online: http://www.cjr.org/issues/2005/1/pein-blog.asp (Accessed February 11, 2006)

Chapter 3

p. 37, Brent Baker and Brent Bozell. *And That's the Way It Isn't.* Alexandria, VA: Media Research Center, 1990, p. 20.

p. 39, Bernard Goldberg. *Bias: A CBS Insider Exposes How the Media Distort the News.* Washington, DC: Regnery Publishing, 2002, p. 18.

p. 40, Goldberg, p. 18.

p. 41, Martin A. Lee, and Norman Solomon, *Unreliable Sources: A Guide to Detecting Bias in News Media.* New York: Carol Publishing Group, 1990, p. 17.

p. 43, Russell Baker, "'Scoops' and Truth at the Times," the *Nation*, June 23, 2003, http://www.thenation.com/docprint.mhtlm?i=20030623 (Accessed December 5, 2005.)

p. 45, Neil Postman. *Amusing Ourselves to Death: Public Discourse in the Age of Show Business.* New York: Penguin Books, 1986, p. 106.

Chapter 4

p. 50, David Brock. *The Republican Noise Machine: Right-Wing Media and How It Corrupts Democracy.* New York: Crown Publishers, 2004, pp. 24–25.

p. 51, David Broder, "Nixon Loyalists Provide Reminders of Era's Dangerous Delusions," the *Washington Post*, June 5, 2005.

p. 51, William Greider. *Who Will Tell the People? The Be-*

trayal of American Democracy. New York: Simon and Schuster, 1992, p. 297.

p. 53, Greider.

p. 55, John Micklethwait and Adrian Wooldridge, *The Right Nation.* New York: Penguin Classics, 2005, p. 90.

Chapter 5

p. 59, D. D. Guttenplan, "Campaign Coverage: Out of It," *Columbia Journalism Review*, July/August 1992, http://archives.cjr.org/year/92/4/perot.asp (Accessed December 8, 2005.)

p. 63, http://www.drudgereport.com/ml.htm (Accessed December 8, 2005.)

Chapter 6

p. 69, Peter Phillips. *Censored 2004: The Top 25 Censored Stories.* New York: Seven Stories Press, 2003, pp. 11–12.

p. 70, Martin A. Lee, and Norman Solomon. *Unreliable Sources: A Guide to Detecting Bias in News Media.* New York: Carol Publishing Group, 1990, pp. 60–61.

p. 70, *Censored 2004: The Top 25 Censored Stories,* p. 27.

p. 79, The Museum of Broadcast Communications, "Fairness Doctrine: U.S. Broadcasting Policy," http://www.museum.tv/archives/etv/F/htmlF/fairnessdoct/fairnessdoct.htm (Accessed July 1, 2005.)

Chapter 7

p. 86, "SouthCom Showdown," *Newsweek*, May 9, 2005, p. 10.

p. 89, Evan Thomas, "How a Fire Broke Out," *Newsweek*, May 23, 2005.

p. 89, L. Brent Bozell, "Newsweek: A Dan Rather Re-run," Media Research Center, May 18, 2005,

http://www.mediaresearch.org/BozellColumns/
newscolumn/2005/col20050518.asp (Accessed
December 10, 2005.)

p. 89, Howard Kurtz, "Debate Over *Newsweek* Retraction of Report Widens," *Washington Post*, May 18, 2005, p. A12.

p. 91, Sidebar: Kenneth A. Paulson, "When Comedy Offends: Revisiting the Smothers Brothers," Freedom forum, November 4, 2001, http://www.freedomforum.org/templates/document.asp? documentID=15292 (Accessed May 23, 2005.)

pp. 92–93, Tom Teepen, "A Skirmish in the Culture War," *Sarasota Herald Tribune*, May 21, 2005, p. 21A.

Chapter 8

p. 98, Martin A. Lee and Norman Solomon. *Unreliable Sources: A Guide to Detecting Bias in News Media.* New York: Carol Publishing Group, 1990, p. 85.

p. 101, Jonathan Chait, "Saving PBS from the GOP," *Los Angeles Times*, May 6, 2005.

p. 101, Eric Boehlert, "Pushing PBS to the Right," *Salon* online magazine, May 10, 2005, http://www.salon.com (Accessed December 10, 2005.)

p. 101, Pat Nason, "Analysis: Liberal Bias at PBS?" *Washington Times*, May 5, 2005 http://washingtontimes.com/ upi-breaking/20050502-051219-5106r.htm (Accessed July 1, 2005.)

Further Information

Anderson, Brian C. *South Park Conservatives: The Revolt Against Liberal Media Bias.* Washington, DC: Regnery Publishing, 2002.

Day, Nancy. *Censorship or Freedom of Expression?* Minneapolis, MN: Lerner, 2001.

Gellman, Mark. *Bad Stuff in the News: A Guide to Handling the Headlines.* New York: SeaStar Books, 2002.

Henderson, Harry. *Power of the News Media.* Library in a Book series. New York: Facts on File, 2004.

Kallen, Stuart. *Media Bias.* At Issue series. San Diego, CA: Greenhaven Press, 2004.

Kuypers, Jim. *Press Bias and Politics: How the Media Frame Controversial Issues.* New York: Praeger, 2002.

Niven, David. *Tilt? The Search for Media Bias.* New York: Praeger, 2002.

Stay, Byron L., ed. *Mass Media.* San Diego, CA: Greenhaven Press, 1999.

Torr, James D., ed. *Is Media Violence a Problem?* San Diego, CA: Greenhaven Press, 2002.

Web Sites

Accuracy in Media
http://www.aim.org/

Center for Media and Democracy
http://www.prwatch.org/

Fairness and Accuracy in Reporting
http://www.fair.org/index.php

Institute for Media, Peace, and Security
http://www.mediapeace.org/

Media Matters for America
http://mediamatters.org/

Newswatch.org
http://www.newswatch.org/

Bibliography

Alexander, Alice, and Jarice Hanson. *Taking Sides: Clashing Views on Controversial Issues in Mass Media and Society.* Guilford, CT: Dushking Publishing Group, 1995.

Alterman, Eric. *What Liberal Media?: The Truth About Bias And The News.* New York: Basic Books, 2003.

Bozell, L. Brent, and Brent H. Baker. *And That's the Way It Isn't: A Reference Guide to Media Bias.* Alexandria, VA: Media Research Center, 1990.

Cook, Timothy. *Governing With the News: The News Media as a Political Institution.* Chicago: The University of Chicago Press, 1998.

Fallows, James. *Breaking the News: How the Media Undermine American Democracy.* New York: Pantheon Books, 1996.

Gans, Herbert. *Deciding What's News: A Study of CBS Evening News, NBC Nightly News, Newsweek & Time.* New York: Pantheon, 1979.

Goldberg, Bernard. *Bias: A CBS Insider Exposes How the Media Distort the News.* Washington, DC: Regnery, 2002.

Goldberg, Jonah. "Big Dumb Lie: Journalists Who Insist There Is No Media Bias Problem Are Just Cutting Themselves Off From The American Public." *The American Enterprise*, July–August 2003, p. 40.

Graham, Tim. *Pattern of Deception.* Alexandria, VA: The Media Research Center, 1996.

Hart, Roderick. *Seducing America: How Television Charms the Modern Voter.* Oxford: The Oxford University Press, 1994.

Lee, Martin A., and Norman Solomon. *Unreliable Sources: A Guide to Detecting Bias in News Media.* New York: Carol Publishing Group, 1990.

Lieberman, Trudy. *Slanting the Story: The Forces That Shape the News.* New York: The New York Press, 2000.

McChesney, Robert. *Rich Media, Poor Democracy: Communication Politics in Dubious Times.* New York: New Press, 2000.

Micklethwait, John, and Adrian Wooldridge. *The Right Nation: Conservative Power in America.* New York: The Penguin Press, 2004.

Niven, David. *Tilt?: The Search For Media Bias.* Westport, CT: Praeger, 2002.

Stay, Byron L., ed. *Mass Media.* San Diego, CA: Greenhaven Press, 1999.

Torr, James D., ed. *Is Media Violence a Problem?* San Diego, CA: Greenhaven Press, 2002.

West, Darrell M. *The Rise and Fall of the Media Establishment.* Boston: St. Martin's Press, 2001.

Index

Page numbers in **boldface** are illustrations.

About the Author

Tom Streissguth has written more than seventy books of nonfiction—including history, geography, and biographies—for young people. Born in Washington D.C., and raised in Minnesota, he attended Yale University and has traveled and studied in Europe, the Middle East, and Asia. He has worked as an editor, teacher, journalist, tour guide, and musician. He currently volunteers as an English-language tutor for immigrants in his hometown of Sarasota, Florida. This is his first book for Marshall Cavendish Benchmark.